D0460175

pocket posh®
christmas logic 5

pocket posh®
christmas logic 5
100 PUZZLES

The Puzzle Society™
puzzlesociety.com

Andrews McMeel
Publishing

Kansas City • Sydney • London

POCKET POSH®
CHRISTMAS LOGIC 5

Andrews McMeel Publishing, LLC
an Andrews McMeel Universal company
1130 Walnut Street, Kansas City, Missouri 64106

14 15 16 17 18 SHZ 10 9 8 7 6 5 4 3 2 1

ISBN: 978-1-4494-5198-1

All puzzles supplied under license from Puzzler Media Ltd.

www.puzzler.com
www.andrewsmcmeel.com
www.puzzlesociety.com

Illustration by Bren Talavera

ATTENTION: SCHOOLS AND BUSINESSES

Andrews McMeel books are available at quantity discounts with bulk purchase for educational, business, or sales promotional use. For information, please e-mail the Andrews McMeel Publishing Special Sales Department: specialsales@amuniversal.com.

HOW TO SOLVE A LOGIC PUZZLE

The introduction sets the scene. Use the chart to record information from the clues. Enter an **✗** for a definite "no" and a **✔** to show a "yes." This process will help to narrow down the possibilities and may eliminate alternatives to provide new information. Return to the clues, in the light of any new facts, to uncover more positive/negative relationships.

Example

Three children live on the same street. From the two clues given below, can you discover each child's full name and age?

Clues
1 Miss Brown is three years older than Mary.
2 The child whose surname is White is 9 years old.

	Brown	Green	White	7	9	10
Anne						
Brian						
Mary						
7						
9						
10						

Anne	Brian	Mary

	Brown	Green	White	7	9	10
Anne	✔	✘	✘	✘	✘	✔
Brian	✘	✘	✔	✘	✔	✘
Mary	✘		✘	✔	✘	✘
7	✘		✘			
9	✘	✘	✔			
10	✔	✘	✘			

	Anne	**Brian**	**Mary**
	Brown	White	Green
	10	9	7

Solution

Miss Brown (clue 1) cannot be Brian. Place an ✘ in the Brian/Brown box. She cannot be Mary, so put an ✘ in the Mary/Brown box. Miss Brown is therefore Anne. Place a ✔ in that box and an ✘ against other possible surnames for Anne.

Anne Brown is three years older than Mary (clue 1). She must be 10 and Mary, 7. Place ✔s in the Anne/10, Brown/10 and Mary/7 boxes. Place ✘s in the empty boxes in each row and column containing these ✔s.

The chart now reveals Brian's age as 9.

Place a ✔ in the Brian/9 box.

Clue 2 states that White is 9, so he must be Brian. Place a ✔ in the White/9 box and Brian/White boxes and an ✘ in each row and column containing these ✔s.

The unfilled boxes must contain ✔s, so Green must be the surname of 7-year-old Mary.

COMPANY FOR CHRISTMAS

Three women from neighboring houses are each having family guests, in the form of a married couple, for Christmas. From the clues given below, can you work out each one's house number and the names of her two guests?

1 The woman from No.13 will have her sister and brother-in-law.

2 May is to entertain her daughter Susan with her husband, who is not Christopher.

3 Roger and his wife are to stay at the house next door to Lill's; Lill will have her cousin to stay.

4 The number of Elsa's house is two less that of the one where David is to stay.

5 Jane will not be at No.11.

	No.11	No.13	No.15	Jane	Susan	Wendy	Christopher	David	Roger
Elsa									
May									
Lill									
Christopher									
David									
Roger									
Jane									
Susan									
Wendy									

Hostess	Number	Female guest	Male guest

Deck the halls

A FINE DAY

Three men had to pay fines at the local library recently when they each returned a borrowed item after the due date. From the clues given below, can you work out the first name and surname of each of the men, what each was returning, and what fine he had to pay?

1 Mr. Andrews was fined $2; Mr. Brown was not returning an overdue book.

2 Brian had kept a DVD for longer than he should.

3 Arthur was fined $1 for keeping his borrowed item a week too long.

4 Charlie Chaplin has spent most of his life living down his famous name.

	Andrews	Brown	Chaplin	Book	CD	DVD	$1	$1.50	$2
Arthur									
Brian									
Charlie									
$1									
$1.50									
$2									
Book									
CD									
DVD									

First name	Surname	Borrowed item	Fine

LET'S FACE IT

Four children were each given a picture of a man's face and invited to adorn it in a different manner. From the clues given below, can you work out the name and age of the child who was given each of pictures 1 to 4, and complete them by drawing in the missing detail in each picture?

1 Picture 2, which is clean-shaven, was produced by the artist a year older than Mary.

2 The oldest child produced picture 1.

3 Silas gave his character a monocle; this picture is somewhere to the right of the one produced by the artist aged 8.

4 Alistair is 9; his picture is not immediately to the right of the one with a mustache.

Names: Alistair; Jennifer; Mary; Silas
Ages: 8; 9; 10; 11
Features: Beard; monocle; mustache; spectacles

Name:	_____	_____	_____	_____
Age:	_____	_____	_____	_____
Feature:	_____	_____	_____	_____

Starting tip: Begin by naming the child aged 11.

with boughs of holly,

SUKO

Enter the numbers 1 to 9 in the spaces so that the number in each circle is equal to the sum of its four surrounding squares. Each colored area should add up to the color totals below.

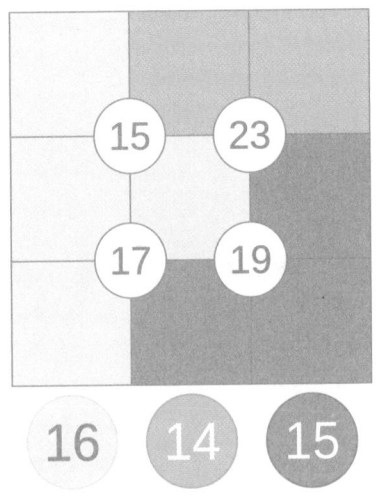

LOGIC 5

EATING OUT

Three couples ate out on different evenings last week. From the clues given below, can you match the pairs, and say where each couple ate out on which day?

1 Harry and Kitty ate out later in the week than the couple who went to the Taj Mahal.
2 Lucinda and her companion went out for a meal later in the week than the couple who visited the Phoenix.
3 Saul and his partner ate at the Golden Goose.

	Kitty	Lucinda	Pearl	Golden Goose	Phoenix	Taj Mahal	Monday	Wednesday	Friday
Harry									
Magnus									
Saul									
Monday									
Wednesday									
Friday									
Golden Goose									
Phoenix									
Taj Mahal									

Male	Female	Restaurant	Evening

Fa la la la la la

YOUNG HOPEFULS

Three guys who were at school together have each been taken on as young players at different soccer teams. From the clues given below, can you identify them and work out the full name of the team each has joined?

1 Evan's surname is not Pass.
2 Lester Cross has not joined Richfield Rowdies.
3 Trapp is on the staff at Middleby, who are not known as the Kickers.

	Cross	Pass	Trapp	Lockstead	Middleby	Richfield	Kickers	Eagles	Rowdies
Delroy									
Evan									
Lester									
Kickers									
Eagles									
Rowdies									
Lockstead									
Middleby									
Richfield									

First name	Surname	Team	Suffix

SOLITARY

It's 1929 and the four solitary confinement cells in America's notorious Rocky Ridge Federal Prison are occupied by convicts who were involved in a fight in the dining hall. From the clues given below, can you work out the name of each cell's occupant, which city he's from, and for what crime he's serving time?

1 Duke Fitzgerald was jailed for running a vicious protection racket—but not in the city of New York.
2 Wolf Levitch, the man from Atlantic City, has a cell numbered one higher than that occupied by the former big-time numbers racketeer.
3 Pistols Crocetti is in cell 4; the convict in cell 2 isn't Rosy Schwartz.
4 The bootlegger comes from Boston, Massachusetts.

	Duke Fitzgerald	Pistols Crocetti	Rosy Schwartz	Wolf Levitch	Atlantic City	Boston	Chicago	New York	Bank robbery	Bootlegging	Numbers racket	Protection racket
Cell 1												
Cell 2												
Cell 3												
Cell 4												
Bank robbery												
Bootlegging												
Numbers racket												
Protection racket												
Atlantic City												
Boston												
Chicago												
New York												

Cell	Name	City	Crime

la la la la,

LOGIC 8

ON SITE

Four couples are having a holiday in their caravans on a popular beach site. From the clues given below, can you name the couple in each of the caravans numbered 1 to 4, and say where each pair is from?

1 Paul's caravan is somewhere to the right of the one being used by Alicia, from Chicago, and her partner.
2 Esme and her partner are separated from Desmond and his partner only by the couple from Boston.
3 Sebastian and Zoe have a lower-numbered caravan than the couple from L.A.
4 Miranda is staying in caravan 3, but not with Luther.

Males: Desmond; Luther; Paul; Sebastian
Females: Alicia; Esme; Miranda; Zoe
Cities: Boston; Chicago; El Paso; Los Angeles

	1	2	3	4
Male:				
Female:				
City:				

Starting tip: Start by naming the woman in caravan 4.

RANKING ORDER

The first three places in a motor race were taken by drivers driving different makes of auto. From the clues given below, can you fully identify the man who finished in each position, and work out which car he was driving?

1 Lopez was driving the Tarantula.

2 The driver of the Rapide finished somewhere ahead of Gus.

3 Bernstein, who is not Karl, was the winner of the race.

4 Potter was not the third-placed driver, and the Cougar did not finish second.

	Chris	Gus	Karl	Bernstein	Lopez	Potter	Cougar	Rapide	Tarantula
First									
Second									
Third									
Cougar									
Rapide									
Tarantula									
Bernstein									
Lopez									
Potter									

Position	First name	Surname	Car

'Tis the season

ABC

Each line, across and down, is to have each of the letters A, B, C, and D, and two empty squares. The letter outside the grid shows the first or second letter in the direction of the arrow. Can you fill in the grid?

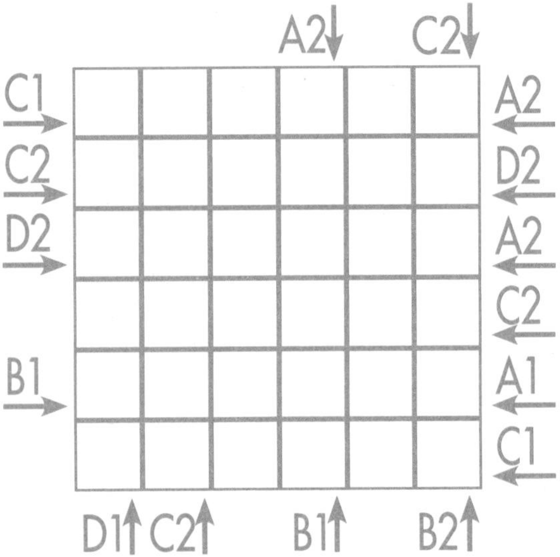

	A2↓		C2↓	

C1 →

C2 →

D2 →

B1 →

A2 ←
D2 ←
A2 ←
C2 ←
A1 ←
C1 ←

D1↑ C2↑ B1↑ B2↑

SMOKE GETS IN YOUR EYES

The picture below shows four members of an army parachute display team practicing for a major event. As he descends, each man triggers a device strapped to his leg that emits brightly colored smoke. From the clues given below, can you work out the rank and surname of each parachutist, and say what color of smoke he is trailing?

1 Allenby, who is trailing green smoke, is immediately ahead of—and below—the captain, whose surname is not Wolfe.

2 Parachutist C is the private.

3 Corporal Havelock, who is not parachutist A, is not trailing red smoke.

4 The sergeant's surname is one letter longer than that of the man who is trailing blue smoke.

Ranks: Captain; corporal; private; sergeant
Surnames: Allenby; Gordon; Havelock; Wolfe
Smoke colors: Blue; green; orange; red

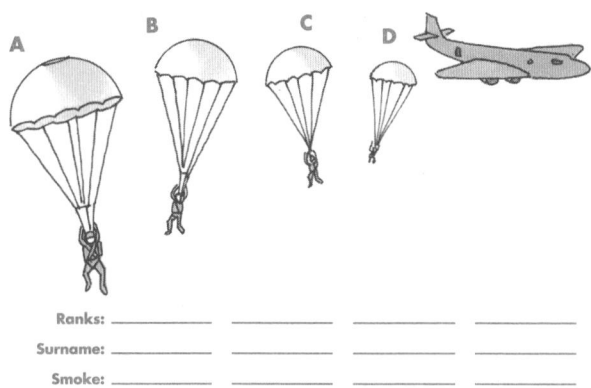

Ranks:	_____	_____	_____	_____
Surname:	_____	_____	_____	_____
Smoke:	_____	_____	_____	_____

Starting tip: Work out the color of the smoke trailing the corporal.

to be jolly,

WORD PLAY

Three friends had a game of Scrabble. From the clues given below, can you work out each one's longest word, best score in one turn, and total number of points?

1 George, whose longest word was not the shortest, had a best score of 18.

2 Mike's longest word was MANNER; his total was not 176.

3 The friend who notched up 24 for his best score did not have a total of 169.

4 John won the game.

	DREADED	GAILY	MANNER	18 points	24 points	36 points	169	176	182
George									
John									
Mike									
169									
176									
182									
18 points									
24 points									
36 points									

Name	Longest word	Best score	Total points

ON THE MOVE

Three brothers, whose father was a Methodist minister in Iowa who changed circuits at regular intervals, were each born in a different town, each followed a different career, and each now lives in a different place. From the clues given below, can you sort out all the details?

1 John is a teacher.
2 Charles was born in Glenwood.
3 The bank manager, who lives in Davenport, is not Samuel, who was not born in Vinton.
4 The brother born in Sioux City does not live in Ames.

	Birth						**Residence**		
	Vinton	Glenwood	Sioux City	Bank manager	Lawyer	Teacher	Davenport	Ames	Waterloo
Charles									
John									
Samuel									
Davenport									
Ames									
Waterloo									
Bank manager									
Lawyer									
Teacher									

Name	Born	Occupation	Residence

Fa la la la la

SUKO

Enter the numbers 1 to 9 in the spaces so that the number in each circle is equal to the sum of its four surrounding squares. Each colored area should add up to the color totals below.

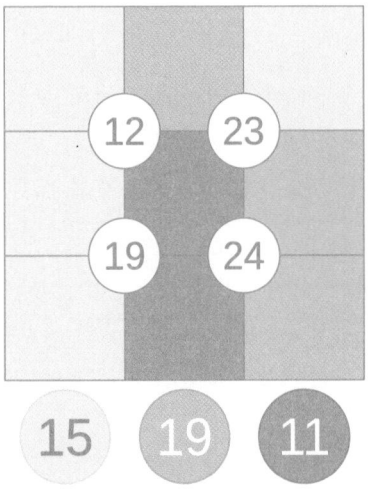

CONVENTION

At the end of October every year, the National Leisure Association takes over a hotel in a beach resort (it's cheaper, out of season) for a big convention, which culminates in a themed fancy dress ball. From the clues given below, can you work out the details of the NLA's conventions over the last four years, the hotel and resort used in each year, and the theme for the ball?

1 The Undercliff Hotel in Longsands, wasn't the venue for NLA's 2012 convention.

2 2010's convention venue was the Pavilion Hotel.

3 The convention at the Metropole Hotel, which isn't in Wairmouth, took place the year before the one where the fancy dress ball had a Wild West theme.

4 In 2013, the theme of the fancy dress ball was Gangsters.

5 The convention in Southbay, where the ball's theme was a Beach Party, was separated by two years from the one at the Grand Hotel.

	Grand	Metropole	Pavilion	Undercliff	Brightbourne	Longsands	Southbay	Wairmouth	Beach Party	Gangsters	Super Heroes	Wild West
2010												
2011												
2012												
2013												
Beach Party												
Gangsters												
Super Heroes												
Wild West												
Brightbourne												
Longsands												
Southbay												
Wairmouth												

Year	Hotel	Resort	Fancy dress

la la la la.

GUESS THE PRICE

The diagram shows four contestants at the table during a recording of the TV quiz show *Guess the Price*. Having been shown an item, each contestant has made a guess as to its price, which is shown on the screen in front of them. From the clues given below, can you work out the full name of the contestant in each of the positions numbered 1 to 4, and work out how much each has estimated the price of the item to be?

1 As viewers look at their TV, David is somewhere to the right of the contestant named Fox; neither of them gave an estimated price of $150.

2 The amount showing in front of the player at either end of the line is not $199.

3 Coney, in position 1, thought that the item was worth more than did his neighbor in position 2.

4 Kevin Mole is somewhere to the left of Joseph as you look at the line-up.

5 Badger's estimate was not $178.

First names: David; Joseph; Kevin; Richard
Surnames: Badger; Coney; Fox; Mole
Amounts: $150; $165; $178; $199

First name: _____ _____ _____ _____

Surname: _____ _____ _____ _____

Amount: _____ _____ _____ _____

Starting tip: Start by working out David's surname.

HORROR BUFFS

Last week Netherlipp's Plaza Cinema showed horror movies in its three studios. On Wednesday, three elderly citizens took advantage of special concessions for pensioners to visit the cinema, each going to a different showing of a different movie. From the clues given below, can you work out which movie each man saw, in which studio it was on, and at what time each performance started?

1 Harry Kirry attended a later performance than the man who saw *The Haunting*, which was not the Studio C movie.
2 Willy Dye went to the Studio B movie, but not for the 6:00 showing.
3 Mac Arborough did not choose *Nightmare*.
4 The man who went to Studio A to see *Return of the Ghouls* did not go for the 8:00 performance.

	Nightmare	Return of the Ghouls	The Haunting	Studio A	Studio B	Studio C	2:30	6:00	8:00
Harry Kirry									
Mac Arborough									
Willy Dye									
2:30									
6:00									
8:00									
Studio A									
Studio B									
Studio C									

Name	Movie	Studio	Time

Don we now

STARLETS

In the heyday of Hollywood, three child stars were contracted to different movie companies. From the clues given below, can you identify the three, work out their respective ages at the time, and say which company each was with?

1 The Warner Brothers starlet was older than Virginia Eidel.

2 Hughie was younger than the starlet named Vedette.

3 Judith's contract was with Paramount.

	Eidel	Starr	Vedette	8	10	12	MGM	Paramount	Warner Bros
Hughie									
Judith									
Virginia									
MGM									
Paramount									
Warner Bros									
8									
10									
12									

First name	Surname	Age	Company

BIRD FOOD

Four members of the Northford Ornithological Society have spent the day in the mountains checking habitats. Naturally, each carried a fortifying flask of steaming coffee, a pack of sandwiches, and a cake. From the clues below, can you work out the full name of each bird-watcher, and say what sort of sandwiches and what kind of cake they ate?

1 The ornithologist who had ham sandwiches has a surname one letter shorter than Dawn's.

2 The forename of the person whose sandwiches contained corned beef immediately precedes that of the doughnut-eater in the alphabetical list.

3 The twitcher who had salami sandwiches has a shorter surname than the one whose cake was a chocolate cake.

4 One of the men had cheese sandwiches and a cupcake.

5 Amy's surname is Pigeon.

	Bunting	Finch	Pigeon	Swan	Cheese	Corned beef	Ham	Salami	Cupcake	Chocolate cake	Danish pastry	Doughnut
Amy												
Bill												
Colin												
Dawn												
Cupcake												
Chocolate cake												
Danish pastry												
Doughnut												
Cheese												
Corned beef												
Ham												
Salami												

First name	Surname	Sandwiches	Cake

our gay apparel,

ABC

Each line, across and down, is to have each of the letters A, B, C, and D, and two empty squares. The letter outside the grid shows the first or second letter in the direction of the arrow. Can you fill in the grid?

	A1↓		B2↓	A2↓		
D2→							←B2
D1→							←B1
C2→							←A2
D1→							←A2
A2→							
D2→							←B2
	B1↑	C1↑	D2↑	B2↑		

LOGIC 21

AT THE WHEEL

When the fair came to town, four young friends went on the bumper cars at the same time. The diagram shows them at the moment when they were heading for a multiple shunt in the center of the arena. From the clues given below, can you work out the full name of the youngster in each of the cars numbered 1 to 4, and say what color it was?

1 The blue car, with Briggs at the wheel, is immediately clockwise round the circuit from the one driven by Lewis.
2 Car 3, which is bright yellow, is driven by one of the boys.
3 Daphne Allen's car is not the red one.
4 The surname of the youngster in car 1 is Grant.
5 Eleanor is driving car number 2.

First names: Daphne; David; Eleanor; Lewis
Surnames: Allen; Briggs; Grant; Powell
Colors of cars: Blue; green; red; yellow

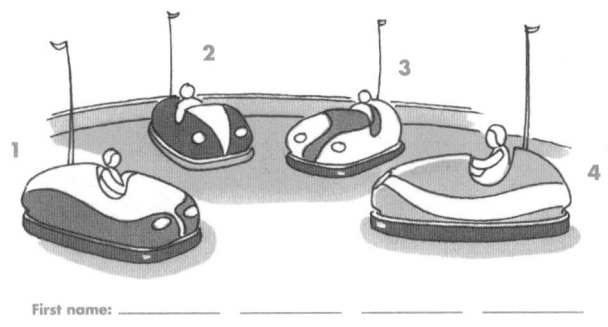

First name: _____ _____ _____ _____
Surname: _____ _____ _____ _____
Color _____ _____ _____ _____

Starting tip: Begin by working out which car Daphne was driving.

Fa la la.

CANINE CLOSE

The families at each of four neighboring houses in Canine Close own dogs of different breeds. From the clues given below, can you say who lives at each of the houses numbered 17 to 23, and name and state the breed of each family's pet?

1 The beagle lives next door to Sam, who belongs to the family named Lead.
2 The pet at No. 17 is the boxer.
3 The Collers own the chihuahua.
4 Freddie's home is at No. 21.
5 The surname of the family at No. 19 is not Kennell.
6 Max is the Yorkshire terrier.

Families: Bone; Coller; Kennell; Lead
Breeds: Beagle; boxer; chihuahua; Yorkshire terrier
Dogs' names: Dick; Freddie; Max; Sam

17	19	21	23

Family: _____ _____ _____ _____
Breed: _____ _____ _____ _____
Name: _____ _____ _____ _____

Starting tip: First work out the breed of Sam.

FROZEN CHOSEN

Three women sitting in the waiting area of a hospital clinic discovered that they all received a weekly supply of frozen meals and compared notes about their favorite main courses and desserts. From the clues given below, can you work out each one's full name and her favorite dishes?

1 Mrs. Lewis's favorite dessert is key lime pie.
2 The woman who prefers jambalaya also has a liking for ice cream; her first name is not Flora.
3 Anne, whose surname is not Barley, does not care for crab cakes.
4 Lorna Hilton's favorite main course is not fried chicken; she avoids apple pie as she thinks it may have too many calories.

	Barley	Hilton	Lewis	Jambalaya	Crab cakes	Fried chicken	Apple pie	Ice cream	Key lime pie
Anne									
Flora									
Lorna									
Apple pie									
Ice cream									
Key lime pie									
Jambalaya									
Crab cakes									
Fried chicken									

First name	Surname	Main course	Dessert

la la la,

SUKO

Enter the numbers 1 to 9 in the spaces so that the number in each circle is equal to the sum of its four surrounding squares. Each colored area should add up to the color totals below.

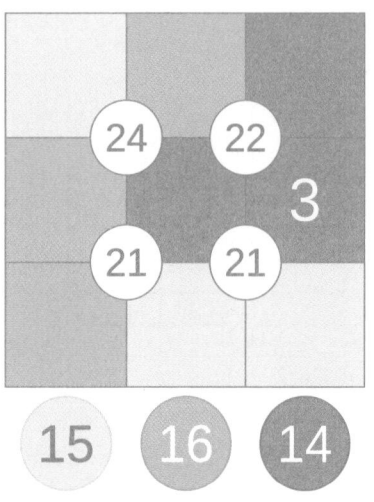

CONSTABLE'S DOGS

A recently discovered painting by English artist John Constable (1776 – 1837) is called *Dedham High Street, With Dogs*. Research has identified all four of the animals shown in the painting. From the clues given below, can you work out the name and breed of each dog, and the name and occupation of its owner?

1 The name of Alfred Banks's dog separates those of the spaniel and the publican's pet in the alphabetical list.

2 The greyhound belonged to Henry Joad.

3 The town laundress's animal was a bulldog.

4 Diamond belonged to the doctor.

5 The midwife did not call her animal Bounce.

6 The name of Gladys Hope's dog is not adjacent to that of the dalmatian in the alphabetical list.

	Bulldog	Dalmatian	Greyhound	Spaniel	Alfred Banks	Gladys Hope	Henry Joad	Mary Newman	Doctor	Laundress	Midwife	Publican
Bounce												
Diamond												
Midget												
Traveler												
Doctor												
Laundress												
Midwife												
Publican												
Alfred Banks												
Gladys Hope												
Henry Joad												
Mary Newman												

Dog's name	Breed	Owner	Occupation

la la la.

VACATION

Three families each decided to vacation in the United States this year. From the clues given below, can you match mothers, fathers, and children, and say which area each family chose to visit?

1 Janice and Ewan are not the couple who visited New York, and their child is not called Adam.

2 Sally went away with her father, Clyde.

3 It was Maxine who went to Florida, but not with Peter.

	Clyde	Ewan	Peter	Adam	Denise	Sally	California	Florida	New York
Janice									
Lucy									
Maxine									
California									
Florida									
New York									
Adam									
Denise									
Sally									

Mother	Father	Child	Area

UFOS OVER UPDOWN

On Saturday night, the police in Updown received calls from local residents who thought they had seen UFOs hovering over different places in the town. It all turned out to be a laser show in the neighboring town of Hilldale. Can you work out from the clues the name and address of the people who rang the police, how they described what they thought they saw, and what they thought it was hovering over?

1 The man who thought he saw a UFO hovering over the Updown District Hospital described a red triangle in the sky.

2 The UFO seen apparently hovering over the town's cemetery wasn't the one said to look like a green disc.

3 Alf Penny was certain he'd seen a "spaceship" in the sky over the town hall.

4 Eva Brick lives in Mill Street; the cube-shaped yellow UFO was reported by the person from Sheep Lane.

5 A resident of One Tree Hill believed there was a UFO over the reservoir on Saturday night.

	Bush Grove	Mill Street	One Tree Hill	Sheep Lane	Green disc	Red triangle	White sphere	Yellow cube	Cemetery	Hospital	Town Hall	Reservoir
Alf Penny												
Eva Brick												
Kitty Catt												
Sean Lamb												
Cemetery												
Hospital												
Town Hall												
Reservoir												
Green disc												
Red triangle												
White sphere												
Yellow cube												

Name	Address	Description	Seen over

Troll the ancient

LAKE DWELLERS

Three couples recently had enjoyable stays beside different Italian lakes. From the clues given below, can you match husbands and wives and say by what lake and in what hotel each couple stayed?

1 David, but not Claire, visited Lake Maggiore.

2 The couple who went to Lake Como stayed at the Splendide.

3 The Bella Vista is not on the shore of Lake Garda.

4 Amanda and Rob did not have a room at the Grand.

	Amanda	Claire	Kate	Como	Garda	Maggiore	Bella Vista	Grand	Spendide
David									
Rob									
Tom									
Bella Vista									
Grand									
Spendide									
Como									
Garda									
Maggiore									

Husband	Wife	Lake	Hotel

HIGHBROW HORROR

A new literary award, the Shooker prize, has recently been instituted for the best piece of horror fiction. As is the custom, last week's first award ceremony, duly televised, was preceded by a discussion of the four short-listed novels by four critics sitting round a table. From the clues given below, can you show by each place in the diagram the name of the critic who sat there and the title of the book he or she thought most worthy of the prize?

1 The critic who favored *Curse of the Mummy* sat next clockwise after Cranleigh Simister and opposite a woman.

2 *Bloodless Butchery* was the choice of the person opposite Dermot Goole.

3 The panel member who preferred *Devil's Picnic* was next clockwise after Deirdre Gore and opposite Gayle Plasmer.

4 *Fiend from Space* got the backing of the critic at D.

Critics: Cranleigh Simister; Deirdre Gore; Dermot Goole; Gayle Plasmer
Titles: *Bloodless Butchery*; *Curse of the Mummy*; *Devil's Picnic*; *Fiend from Space*

Critic: ——————— B
Title: ———————
C
Critic: ———————
Title: ———————
A
Critic: ———————
Title: ———————
D
Critic: ———————
Title: ———————

Starting tip: Work out who chose *Curse of the Mummy.*

Yule tide carol,

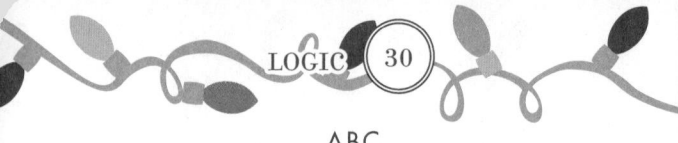

ABC

Each line, across and down, is to have each of the letters A, B, C, and D, and two empty squares. The letter outside the grid shows the first or second letter in the direction of the arrow. Can you fill in the grid?

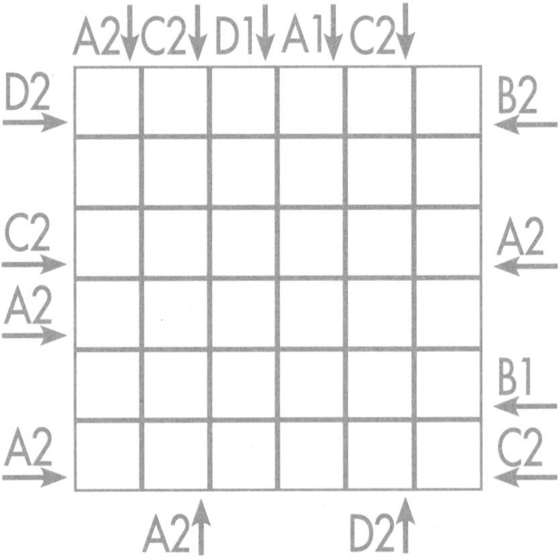

A2↓ C2↓ D1↓ A1↓ C2↓

D2→   ←B2

C2→   ←A2

A2→

       ←B1

A2→   ←C2

A2↑   D2↑

A LITTLE BIT EXTRA

Four aspiring actresses have been filling in their time by doing "extra" work at the famous Larchwood Studios and each makes her first appearance on screen in a newly released movie. From the clues given below, can you work out how long each of them is actually visible, the role she's playing, and the title of the movie?

1 The name of the actress seen in *Plain Clothes* immediately follows in the alphabetical list of the one who is on screen for 47 seconds as a hospital nurse.

2 Donna Essex, who plays a cab driver, is visible for a shorter period than the actress who's an extra in *Bad Company*.

3 Angie Bruce makes the shortest screen appearance of all, but not as a uniformed air hostess.

4 No receptionist appears, however briefly, in the foreground or the background, in *High Flyers*.

	17 seconds	29 seconds	47 seconds	54 seconds	Air hostess	Cab driver	Nurse	Receptionist	Bad Company	Green Sun	High Flyers	Plain Clothes
Angie Bruce												
Donna Essex												
Gail Hatton												
Julie Kirby												
Bad Company												
Green Sun												
High Flyers												
Plain Clothes												
Air hostess												
Cab driver												
Nurse												
Receptionist												

Actress	Screen time	Role	Movie

Fa la la la la,

LOGIC 32

ISLAND IN THE SUN

The diagram shows a small Caribbean island that has developed recently as a tourist center, with its four main towns, situated in locations A to D around the coastline, each offering a special attraction of a different nature to visitors. From the clues given below, can you name each town, say which family was staying there during the week in question, and name the special facility on offer there?

1 The Rhodes family stayed in a hotel in Kingsville, which is next clockwise round the coastline from the town with the marina.

2 The Lesters were accommodated in the east coast resort, while the Barratts stayed in the resort with the pleasure beach.

3 The west coast resort is Whitesands.

4 The casino is in Blue Bay, which is not where the Wardle family was staying.

Resorts: Blue Bay; Kingsville; Nelson; Whitesands
Families: Barratt; Lester; Rhodes; Wardle
Facilities: Casino; marina; pleasure beach; scuba diving center

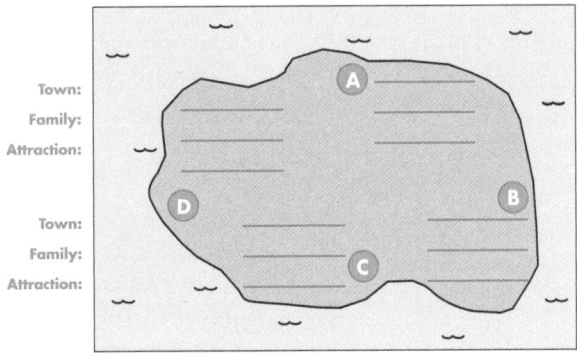

Town:
Family:
Attraction:

Town:
Family:
Attraction:

Starting tip: Begin by naming Kingsville's attraction.

THE WAY TO WORK

Three friends who work for the same firm each travel a different distance to work, and each uses a different form of transport. From the clues given below, can you say what each does, how far away each lives, and how each travels?

1 Jason, the storeman, does not have as long a journey to work as his friend who comes by train.

2 Dennis travels to work on the bus.

3 The clerk makes the 18-mile journey twice every day.

4 Tony is not the firm's accountant.

	Accountant	Clerk	Storeman	15 miles	18 miles	20 miles	Bus	Car	Train
Dennis									
Jason									
Tony									
Bus									
Car									
Train									
15 miles									
18 miles									
20 miles									

Name	Job	Distance	Method

la la la la.

SUKO

Enter the numbers 1 to 9 in the spaces so that the number in each circle is equal to the sum of its four surrounding squares. Each colored area should add up to the color totals below.

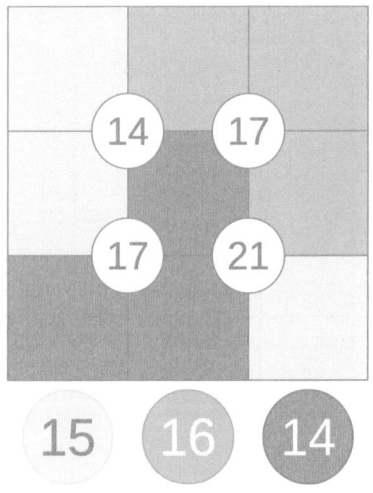

SPLASH

Felicity Fisch is a stuntperson for the movie industry—but one with a speciality: while other stuntpersons are being hit by cars, blown up, and thrown through windows, Felicity just falls into water—though usually, it must be admitted, from a considerable height. From the clues given below, can you work out the details of the last four movies she worked on—what character she was portraying, what she fell from, and what she fell into?

1 In the comedy *Blue Skies*, Felicity had to fall into a cold and none-too-clean Amsterdam canal.

2 For one movie, Felicity takes the part of a female vampire who, hit by the rays of the rising sun, falls from a bridge.

3 Felicity's fall in the thriller *Get Lucky* isn't from a hotel balcony.

4 The scene in which, dressed as a bride, Felicity dives into a river, does not involve a helicopter.

5 *Walkover*, the movie in which Felicity appears as a nurse, isn't the one in which she falls 40 feet from a pier into the sea below.

	Bride	Nurse	Policewoman	Vampire	Balcony	Bridge	Helicopter	Pier	Canal	Lake	River	Sea
Blue Skies												
Get Lucky												
Outsiders												
Walkover												
Canal												
Lake												
River												
Sea												
Balcony												
Bridge												
Helicopter												
Pier												

Movie	Role	Falls from	Fall into

See the blazing

BLOCK PARTY

Home-baking is the order of the day when three women from an apartment block have their weekly get-together, each playing hostess in turn. From the clues given below, can you work out who did the entertaining on the last three meetings, what she served, and in what numbered apartment each woman lives?

1 The woman from No. 15 has a special recipe for cupcakes.

2 May, who did not produce fruit cake, was the hostess the week after her friend from No. 24.

3 Aileen baked some excellent cookies.

4 Gertrude did the entertaining on the 9th; the 23rd was not the turn of the occupant of apartment 7.

	9th	16th	23rd	Fruit cake	Cookies	Cupcakes	No. 7	No. 15	No. 24
Aileen									
Gertrude									
May									
No. 7									
No. 15									
No. 24									
Fruit cake									
Cookies									
Cupcakes									

Woman	Date	Delicacy	Apartment no.

ARTISTIC INTERPRETATIONS

Three artists have been commissioned by their local council to produce a piece for display. From the clues, can you work out the medium and subject of each artist's work and the city in which they live?

1 Graphael, who is not a photographer, had flowers as the subject of his piece of art.

2 Fashion was naturally featured by the artist in Milan.

3 Michelcarlo is the sculptor, but did not use ice cream as his medium. The ice cream artwork was commissioned by the city of Naples.

	Painter	Photographer	Sculptor	Milan	Naples	Rome	Fashion	Flowers	Ice cream
Davido									
Graphaelo									
Michelcarlo									
Fashion									
Flowers									
Ice cream									
Milan									
Naples									
Rome									

Name	Medium	Subject	City

Yule before us,

MY MUSIC

Three teachers at the same school are all lovers of different types of music. From the clues given below, can you identify the three, name each one's teaching subject, and describe their musical tastes?

1 Cassandra's subject is Spanish, but her musical tastes do not run to jazz.
2 Douglas does not teach math.
3 The English teacher is a classical music buff.
4 The pop music fan's surname is Jones.
5 Daniel's surname is not Parnell.

	Douglas	Jones	Parnell	English	Math	Spanish	Classical	Jazz	Pop
Cassandra									
Daniel									
Linda									
Classical									
Jazz									
Pop									
English									
Math									
Spanish									

First name	Surname	Subject	Music

OUTSIDERS IN

Time was when the villagers of Hydebound regarded anyone born more than five miles away as a foreigner, but in the last year four real foreigners have moved in and taken up important positions in the little community. From the clues given, can you work out each one's full name, where they're from, and what they've become in Hydebound?

1 Bernard, who comes from the town of Williwonka in Australia, has a surname one letter shorter than that of Diana, who has taken over as the village's doctor.

2 The new clerk to Hydebound Council has a longer forename than the person who took over as priest; the newcomer who is the same gender as the priest isn't a Canadian.

3 The New Zealander and the recently appointed teacher of Hydebound School, who isn't Cherry, are of the same gender; Cherry's surname isn't Scott.

4 Alastair Houghton's grandfather came from Hydebound, so he considers that he has simply returned to his roots; the villagers still, however, think he's foreign.

	Dugdale	Houghton	Newton	Scott	Australia	Canada	New Zealand	England	Doctor	Teacher	Clerk	Priest
Alastair												
Bernard												
Cherry												
Diana												
Doctor												
Teacher												
Clerk												
Priest												
Australia												
Canada												
New Zealand												
England												

First name	Surname	Country of origin	Job

Fa la la la la,

ABC

Each line, across and down, is to have each of the letters A, B, C, and D, and two empty squares. The letter outside the grid shows the first or second letter in the direction of the arrow. Can you fill in the grid?

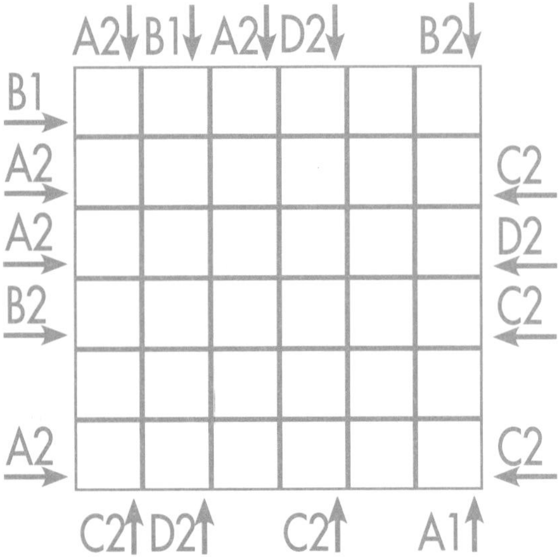

A2↓ B1↓ A2↓ D2↓   B2↓

B1→

A2→   C2←

A2→   D2←

B2→   C2←

A2→   C2←

C2↑ D2↑   C2↑   A1↑

SKATING ON THICK ICE

During a period of severe frost four young women went skating on a park lake (after it had been cleared as safe by the powers that be). From the clues given below, can you fully identify the skaters numbered 1 to 4 in the diagram, and work out the color of the scarf each was wearing as a protection against the cold wind?

1 Bernice High can be seen somewhere to the right of her friend wearing the yellow scarf as you look at the diagram.

2 The skater named Short is wearing the red scarf.

3 The skater wearing the green scarf is somewhere to the left of Louise in the diagram.

4 The blue scarf belongs to the skater in position 1.

5 Jackie, whose surname is not Long, is not in position 2.

Skaters: Bernice; Charlotte; Jackie; Louise
Surnames: High; Little; Long; Short
Scarves: Blue; green; red; yellow

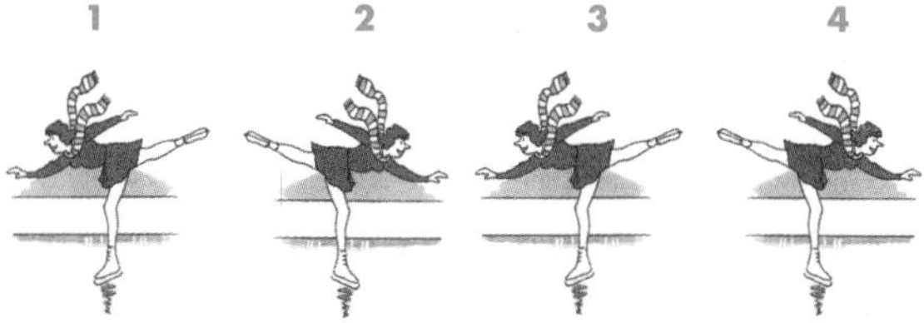

	1	2	3	4
Skater:				
Surname:				
Scarf:				

Starting tip: Start by working out the color of the scarf worn by Bernice.

la la la la.

WORKING HOLIDAY 1

In the United Kingdom lots of people have to work over Christmas—nurses, police officers, reindeers—and some London criminals choose to do it too, as it gives them plenty of time to tunnel into secure premises. From the clues given below, can you work out what sort of business each of the listed villains is working on this year, where it is, and which way he's going in?

1 "Ginger" Hood is cutting his way through the side wall of one building.

2 The man who's tunneling through the floor from the sewers into a set of South London business premises, which do not belong to the bullion dealers, isn't "Spider" Turpin.

3 The art gallery being robbed is in West London.

4 The North London business targeted by "Rocky" Sikes isn't the bank that is being entered through the back wall.

	Art gallery	Bank	Bullion dealer	Jewelers	East London	North London	South London	West London	Back wall	Floor	Roof	Side wall
"Ginger" Hood												
"Ozzy" Peace												
"Rocky" Sikes												
"Spider" Turpin												
Back wall												
Floor												
Roof												
Side wall												
East London									
North London									
South London									
West London									

Crook	Target	Location	Entry route

WORKING HOLIDAY 2

While the four crooks are working away over Christmas as described in the previous problem, their wives and children are involved in the nativity play being staged by St. Moriarty's Church. From the clues given below, can you work out what role in the production each wife took, the name of her child, and the child's part in the play?

1 Helen Hood's daughter Rebecca isn't playing an ox or a shepherd; the shepherd's mother was in charge of the refreshments.

2 Clive's surname isn't Turpin; Helen Hood can't play any musical instrument.

3 Patsy Peace's offspring is playing Caspar, one of the Wise Men.

4 Matthew's mom, who isn't Patsy Peace, is in charge of costumes.

5 Sue Sikes's child has been cast as an animal.

	Costumes	Playing piano	Prompter	Refreshments	Clive	Louisa	Matthew	Rebecca	Donkey	Ox	Shepherd	Wise Man
Helen Hood												
Patsy Peace												
Sue Sikes												
Tracy Turpin												
Donkey									
Ox									
Shepherd									
Wise Man									
Clive					
Louisa					
Matthew					
Rebecca					

Mother	Mother's role	Child	Part

Strike the harp

MONOPOLIZE

Four players are seated round a small table in the positions numbered 1 to 4, playing a game of Monopoly. From the clues given below, can you name the player in each position, work out the total she has thrown on the round just completed, and say which section on the board each has landed on as a result?

1 Alicia, who landed on the Go to Jail square, is seated next clockwise round the table from the player whose two dice totaled five.

2 The player in seat 2 is Eileen; she did not reach Boardwalk on her last throw, which was a higher total than that of Kelly, who is not in seat 4.

3 Rachel shook a total of nine at her last turn.

4 The player in position 3 landed on the Waterworks.

Players: Alicia; Eileen; Kelly; Rachel
Totals: 3; 5; 8; 9
Sections reached: Vermont Avenue; Go to Jail; Boardwalk; Waterworks

Name: ——————   ——————
Total: ——————
Section: ——————

Name: ——————
Total: ——————
Section: ——————
——————
——————
——————

Starting tip: Begin by working out on which section Eileen landed.

HORROR HOLDUPS

There were traffic problems on three successive days in downtown Netherlipp last week. From the clues given below, can you work out what caused the obstruction each day, what time it started, and how long each took to clear?

1 The accident occurred the day before the delay lasting two hours.

2 The one-hour hold-up started at 4:00 p.m.

3 Tuesday's delay lasted longer than the one caused by the 11:00 a.m. mishap, which was not the shedding of a load from a truck.

4 The water main burst was earlier in the day than the problem on Thursday.

	Accident	Burst water main	Shed load	9:00 a.m.	11:00 a.m.	4:00 p.m.	One hour	Two hours	Three hours
Tuesday									
Wednesday									
Thursday									
One hour									
Two hours									
Three hours									
9:00 a.m.									
11:00 a.m.									
4:00 p.m.									

Day	Cause	Time	Time to clear

and join the chorus.

SUKO

Enter the numbers 1 to 9 in the spaces so that the number in each circle is equal to the sum of its four surrounding squares. Each colored area should add up to the color totals below.

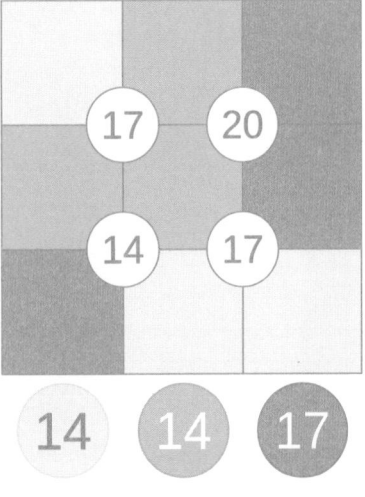

IN THE PICTURE

Three actors of the classic Hollywood era were each involved in a movie being shot over the same period of time. From the clues given below, can you name the three, and describe the role each played, and the genre of movie in which each was a character?

1 Calvin played the role of a cab driver.

2 Norbert Spenlow was not cast in the Western movie.

3 Marchant played the part of a doctor.

4 Dreyfus had star billing in the comedy movie.

	Dreyfus	Marchant	Spenlow	Cab driver	Doctor	Photographer	Comedy	Romance	Western
Calvin									
Norbert									
Willard									
Comedy									
Romance									
Western									
Cab driver									
Doctor									
Photographer									

First name	Surname	Role	Movie

Fa la la la la,

FAIR ENOUGH

Women presenters on Balonian television like to think it enhances their allure, and therefore their career prospects, to dye their hair and become blondes. Take just three of the many: From the clues given below, can you work out their full names, on what channel each appears, and what natural hair color they have, with limited success, tried to disguise?

1 The parting in Dorka's hair reveals that her natural color is black.

2 The surname of the channel 10 presenter is Voshova.

3 The presenter whose hair reveals auburn roots is not on channel 9; she is not Miss Kolorova, whose first name is not Enya.

4 The channel 8 presenter has not completely obliterated her original brown color; Marita's channel has a lower number than that of the colleague whose surname is Rinzova.

	Kolorova	Rinzova	Voshova	Channel 8	Channel 9	Channel 10	Auburn	Black	Brown
Dorka									
Enya									
Marita									
Auburn									
Black									
Brown									
Channel 8									
Channel 9									
Channel 10									

First name	Surname	Channel	Hair color

THE PROTAGONISTS

A page in the front of a new nonfiction spy book carries portraits of the four central characters. From the clues given, can you complete the captions by working out each man's forename and surname?

1 One of the four men is named Maxwell Bernard.

2 The man in picture B is Mr. Lewis, while Neville is shown in the bottom half of the page; the latter's surname is not Percy.

3 Picture A shows neither Duncan nor Eustace; the latter is the surname of one of the protagonists.

4 Percy is pictured immediately to the left of Gregory; one of these names is a first name, the other a surname.

Names: Bernard; Duncan, Eustace; Gregory; Lewis, Maxwell; Neville; Percy.

THE PROTAGONISTS

First name: ———
Surname: ———

First name: ———
Surname: ———

Starting tip: Work out which is the picture of Maxwell.

la la la la.

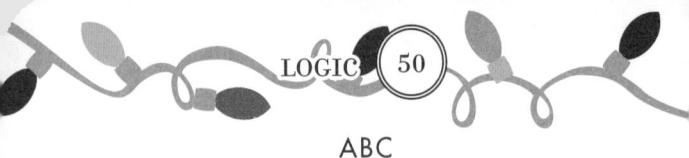

ABC

Each line, across and down, is to have each of the letters A, B, C, and D, and two empty squares. The letter outside the grid shows the first or second letter in the direction of the arrow. Can you fill in the grid?

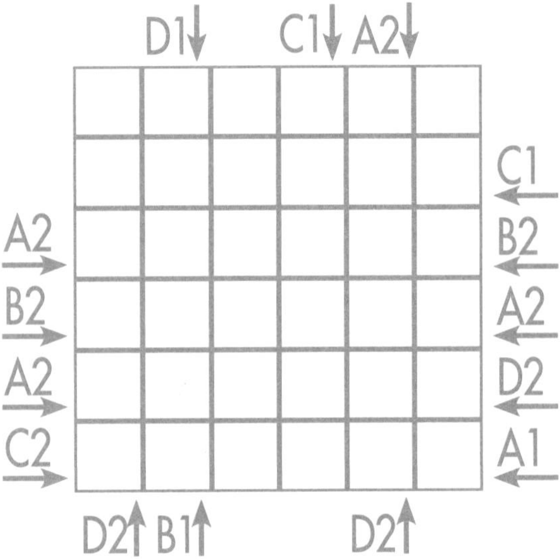

CAPITAL PHOTOS

The diagram shows two pages from Anna's photo album, on which are displayed four photos of female relatives taken while they were on vacation in various European capital cities. From the clues given below, can you work out the relationship and name of the person in each of the photos numbered 1 to 4, and say where each snap was taken?

1 The picture taken in Paris is immediately below the one of Anna's sister.

2 Abigail appears in the shot to the right of the one taken in Athens.

3 Lindsay is Anna's daughter.

4 The picture taken in Brussels bears an even number in the diagram.

5 Anna's cousin's photo, taken in Rome, is indicated by a number one higher than the snap featuring Judith.

Relationships: Aunt; cousin; daughter; sister
Names: Abigail; Judith; Lindsay; Madeleine
Capitals: Athens; Brussels; Paris; Rome

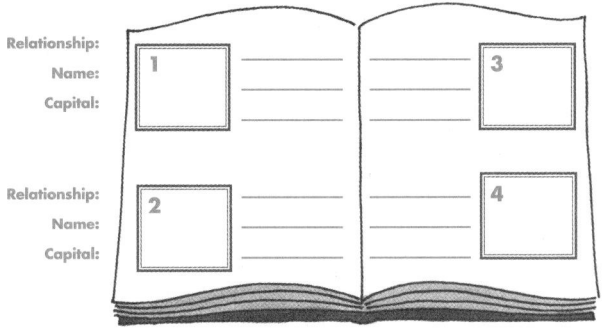

Relationship:
Name:
Capital:

1

3

Relationship:
Name:
Capital:

2

4

Starting tip: First work out where picture 3 was taken.

Follow me

HORSE SENSE

Three girls each own a pony of a different color. From the clues given below, can you work out each girl's full name, and the name and color of the pony she owns?

1 Belinda owns the brown pony, whose name is not Venus.
2 The black pony is owned by the girl whose surname is Hocks.
3 The gray pony's name is Bonnie.
4 Felicity's surname is Withers.

	Hocks	Mayne	Withers	Bonnie	Pandora	Venus	Black	Brown	Gray
Belinda									
Camilla									
Felicity									
Black									
Brown									
Gray									
Bonnie									
Pandora									
Venus									

First name	Surname	Pony	Color

PETLOVERS

Petlovers is a quarterly magazine for—well, petlovers. Each issue has on its cover a picture of a petlover and their pet. From the clues given below, can you work out the details of the cover pictures that have been or will be used for this year's issues—the month of issue, name of the petlover, and name and type of the creature?

1 The lady on the front of the February issue of *Petlovers* is cuddling her Blue Persian cat.

2 Poopsie will be on the cover of the issue that will appear between the one featuring Rose Busch and her pet and the one showing the lady with the Flemish Giant rabbit.

3 Hodge and Pearl Diver, his owner, will be on the cover of the next *Petlovers* after the one featuring Cherub.

4 Alice Springs will be on the front of the May magazine; her pet is not the gerbil.

	Alice Springs	Coral Reef	Pearl Diver	Rose Busch	Cherub	Hodge	Nigel	Poopsie	Cat	Gerbil	Parrot	Rabbit
February												
May												
August												
November												
Cat												
Gerbil												
Parrot												
Rabbit												
Cherub												
Hodge												
Nigel												
Poopsie												

Issue	Owner	Pet name	Animal

in merry measure,

SUKO

Enter the numbers 1 to 9 in the spaces so that the number in each circle is equal to the sum of its four surrounding squares. Each colored area should add up to the color totals below.

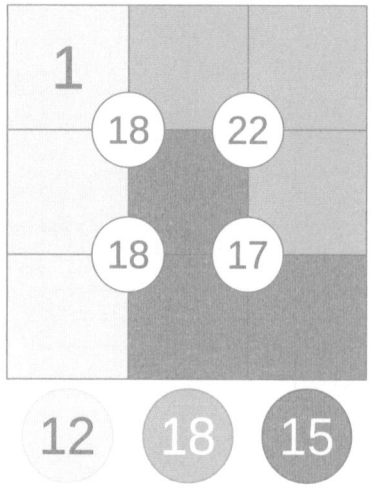

LONG SERVICE

Yesterday, as on all weekdays, three stalwart ladies stood at their usual stations at the service counter of the college cafeteria. From the clues given below, can you work out their names, ages, years of service, and respective responsibilities?

1 The 54-year-old has not been doing the job as long as Nell.

2 The lady who serves the main course is 56.

3 Lottie, who does not dispense the drinks, has 18 years experience.

4 Bridget's responsibility is the dessert.

	52	54	56	16 years	18 years	20 years	Main course	Dessert	Drinks
Bridget									
Lottie									
Nell									
Main course									
Dessert									
Drinks									
16 years									
18 years									
20 years									

Name	Age	Years service	Responsibility

Fa la la,

OUT FOR A RIDE

Four members of a pony club were out for a ride. The diagram shows them riding in single file along a local country trail. From the clues given below, can you name each of the ponies numbered 1 to 4, and fully identify their riders?

1 Buttercup is immediately behind the pony being ridden by Loretta, whose surname is not Mayne.

2 Jennifer is riding Bluebell.

3 Daisy is bringing up the rear in position 4.

4 Melanie Hoofe is in an even-numbered position in the line.

5 The girl named Withers is somewhere in front of the pony called Cowslip.

Ponies: Bluebell; Buttercup; Cowslip; Daisy
Riders: Alison; Jennifer; Loretta; Melanie
Surnames: Hock; Hoofe; Mayne; Withers.

1	2	3	4

Pony: _____ _____ _____ _____
First name: _____ _____ _____ _____
Surname: _____ _____ _____ _____

Starting tip: Start by naming pony 1.

REMAINS OF THE DAY

Four members of the English Northchester Amateur Archaeological Association spent the month of July digging around the site of the former Skandergate Bar. However, they didn't find much; from the clues given below, can you work out when each find was made, who made it, what it was, and the period from which it dated?

1 Fran Grubb made her find, which wasn't of Roman origin, on July 6th.

2 Eric Diggs made his discovery in the first half of July, while the brooch was found in the second half of the month.

3 The World War II landmine was found in the same week as Ann Burrow's find; Ms. Burrow's discovery came on the same day of the week—though not, of course, the same date—as that of the hoard of coins.

4 The Saxon item, which was not a helmet, was uncovered on July 2nd.

	Ann Burrow	Cary Delve	Eric Diggs	Fran Grubb	Brooch	Coins	Helmet	Landmine	Roman	Saxon	Viking	World War II
Monday 2nd												
Friday 6th												
Monday 16th												
Friday 20th												
Roman												
Saxon												
Viking												
World War II												
Brooch												
Coins												
Helmet												
Landmine												

Date	Archaeo-logist	Find	Period

la la la,

WINTER BREAKS

Three friends who went on winter vacations to ski resorts in different countries were each unfortunate enough to have a fall, incurring a break in a different part of their anatomy. From the clues given below, can you fully identify the three and say who went where and broke what?

1 Pearl spent her skiing vacation in the French Alps.
2 The woman who went to Austria broke a leg.
3 The Swiss Alps was not the vacation area chosen by Mrs. Stubbs, who did not break her arm.
4 Sonia's injury was a broken collarbone; her surname is not Tripp.

	Fell	Stubbs	Tripp	Austria	France	Switzerland	Arm	Collarbone	Leg
Delia									
Pearl									
Sonia									
Arm									
Collarbone									
Leg									
Austria									
France									
Switzerland									

First name	Surname	Country	Injury

SPORTS COVERAGE

In September every year *Sportswatch*, a monthly magazine, announces which of the sportsmen who have graced the covers of its last twelve issues has been voted Supersportsman of the Year by readers. From the clues given below, can you work out who took the first four places in last year's competition, his sport, and when he was on the magazine cover?

1 Second place went to the sportsman who was on the cover of the May 2014 issue.

2 The archer was on the magazine cover three months before the title-winner and six months earlier than Danny Evans.

3 Gary Handy finished immediately behind the orienteering champion in the Supersportsman poll.

4 Motocross rider Marcus Nash was placed immediately behind the man from the November 2013 magazine cover.

	Danny Evans	Gary Handy	Marcus Nash	Sam Tomkins	Archery	Lugeing	Motocross	Orienteering	November 2013	February 2014	May 2014	August 2014
First												
Second												
Third												
Fourth												
November 2013												
February 2014												
May 2014												
August 2014												
Archery												
Lugeing												
Motocross												
Orienteering												

Position	Name	Sport	Magazine date

la la la.

ABC

Each line, across and down, is to have each of the letters A, B, C, and D, and two empty squares. The letter outside the grid shows the first or second letter in the direction of the arrow. Can you fill in the grid?

C2↓ D2↓ C2↓ B1↓ C2↓ B2↓

A1→

A2→

D1→

D2↑ B2↑ D2↑ D2↑

D2←

C2←

A2←

B2←

C1←

ADVENTURERS

An article in today's *Northchester Chronicle* features four people from that city who have recently enjoyed some adventurous experiences as a result of being given special gift vouchers from a well-known store as birthday gifts by their partners. From the clues given below, can you work out each person's full name and occupation, and what it was they did?

1 It was the police officer who made a tandem parachute jump over the fields west of the city.

2 Robert, whose surname isn't Collier, fulfilled a lifelong ambition to go scuba diving.

3 Heather is surnamed Walters, but the bus driver's surname isn't Hancock.

4 Martin is a librarian who very seldom gets the chance to do anything adventurous.

5 It wasn't Collier, the real estate agent, who got to fly a glider.

	Collier	Hancock	Scott	Walters	Bus driver	Real estate agent	Librarian	Police officer	Drove race car	Flew glider	Parachute jump	Went scuba diving
Amanda												
Heather												
Martin												
Robert												
Drove race car												
Flew glider												
Parachute jump												
Went scuba diving												
Bus driver												
Real estate agent												
Librarian												
Police officer												

First name	Surname	Occupation	Activity

While I tell

THE LONG AND THE SHORT OF IT

The characters numbered 1 to 4 in the diagram are directors of the local soccer team, and are depicted in the front row of the directors' box at an important end-of-season home match. From the clues given below, can you fully identify and describe each of the four?

1 Clive, who is not chairman of the board, and Broad are neighbors in the box.

2 Ryan, the building contractor, is not in seat 1.

3 Peter is not the large-scale auto retailer, who is not sitting in position 2.

4 As you view the directors' box from the field, Short, the media personality, is immediately to the left of Brendan, and Large is immediately to the right of Long.

First names: Brendan; Clive; Peter; Ryan
Surnames: Broad; Large; Long; Short
Descriptions: Accountant; building contractor; auto retailer; media personality

CHAIRMAN

First name: _____ _____ _____ _____

Surname: _____ _____ _____ _____

Description: _____ _____ _____ _____

Starting tip: First work out the surname of the man in seat 4.

NATIVITY PLAY

Three girls had parts of varying importance in the elementary school's nativity play. From the clues given below, can you identify them, say which part each played, and work out whose class she was in?

1 Sinita Kochar was not the girl cast as a sheep in the flock tended by the shepherds.
2 The girl who took the role of an angel in the nativity play was not called Helen, and she was not in Miss Hughes's class.
3 Miss Greaves was the class teacher of the girl named Maloney.
4 Pearl is in Mrs. Slater's class.

	Abbott	Kochar	Maloney	Angel	Mary	Sheep	Miss Greaves	Miss Hughes	Mrs. Slater
Helen									
Pearl									
Sinita									
Miss Greaves									
Miss Hughes									
Mrs. Slater									
Angel									
Mary									
Sheep									

First name	Surname	Part	Teacher

of Yule tide treasure,

SUKO

Enter the numbers 1 to 9 in the spaces so that the number in each circle is equal to the sum of its four surrounding squares. Each colored area should add up to the color totals below.

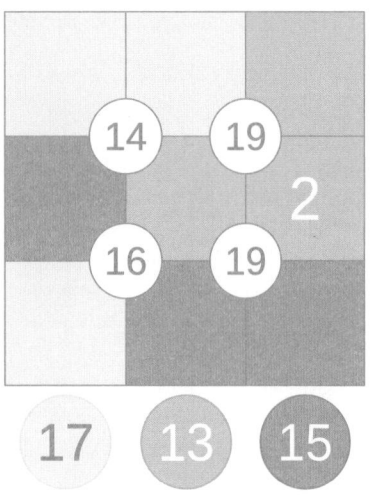

RESTRAINT

Four residents were out walking their dogs one evening and, by chance, were each passing one of a line of four lampposts along the street, numbered 1 to 4 in the diagram. Each managed to persuade his pet not to dally, despite the temptation. From the clues given below, can you name and describe the dog just passing each lamppost, and name his owner?

1 Max, the Welsh terrier, is passing the lamppost immediately behind the one Jack's pet is studiously avoiding.
2 Ernie's dog is Tommy, who is not the boxer.
3 The dog at lamppost 4 does not belong to Dennis.
4 Nicko is just passing lamppost 3 with a nostalgic sniff.
5 Frank's pet is the German Shepherd.

Dogs' names: Bruce; Max; Nicko; Tommy
Breeds: German Shepherd; boxer; Sealyham; Welsh terrier
Owners: Dennis; Ernie; Frank; Jack

Dog's name: _____ _____ _____ _____
Breed: _____ _____ _____ _____
Owner: _____ _____ _____ _____

Starting tip: First name Max's owner.

Fa la la la la,

SERENDIPITY

Three youngsters each found a small coin in a different location the other day. From the clues given below, can you say how old each child is, and work out which coin each found in which location?

1 Wesley found a coin with a higher value than the one found in the park, whose finder was older than him.

2 It was Amanda who found a quarter, but not in the parking lot.

3 The 6-year-old's discovery was lying on the sidewalk.

	5	6	7	Nickle	Dime	Quarter	Parking lot	Park	Sidewalk
Amanda									
Joseph									
Wesley									
Parking lot									
Park									
Sidewalk									
Nickle									
Dime									
Quarter									

Name	Age	Coin	Location

LEFT BEHIND

The diagram shows four adjacent areas at a kennel, in each of which is housed a dog whose owners have gone abroad for a winter European vacation. From the clues given below, can you name and describe the dog in each of the enclosures lettered A to D, and say where its owners have gone?

1 The dog whose owners are in Cyprus is housed next door to Bugsy, the Airedale.

2 Andy has enclosure C; the owners of the dog in the neighboring enclosure D are not in Tenerife.

3 Enclosure B is the temporary home of the Labrador.

4 Bella's owners have flown off to Madeira.

5 The cocker spaniel belongs to the couple enjoying the winter sunshine in Crete.

Dogs' names: Andy; Bella; Bugsy; Mick
Breeds: Airedale; cocker spaniel; Dalmatian; Labrador
Holiday locations: Crete; Cyprus; Madeira; Tenerife

	A	B	C	D

Dog's name:	_____	_____	_____	_____
Breed:	_____	_____	_____	_____
Vacation location:	_____	_____	_____	_____

Starting tip: First find out where Bugsy's owners have gone.

la la la la.

ABC

Each line, across and down, is to have each of the letters A, B, C, and D, and two empty squares. The letter outside the grid shows the first or second letter in the direction of the arrow. Can you fill in the grid?

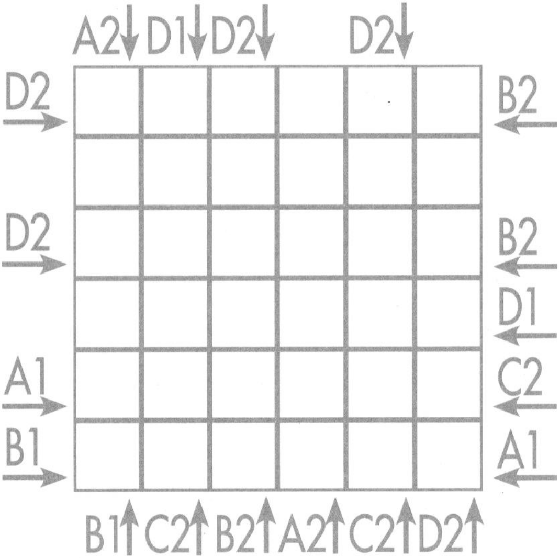

A2↓ D1↓ D2↓   D2↓

D2→

B2←

D2→

B2←

D1←

A1→

C2←

B1→

A1←

B1↑ C2↑ B2↑ A2↑ C2↑ D2↑

SEEDY GROVE

Three residents of Cedar Grove are in the hospital at the moment and were last night visited by neighbors. From the clues given below, can you work out which patient is in which ward and was visited by which neighboring couple from which number house?

1 Mr. Cropper was visited by the couple from No. 26.

2 Mrs. Fell is a patient in ward 39.

3 The Dohertys have the next higher house number after the couple who spent some time in ward 53, which is not Mrs. Downes's ward.

4 The Saxenbys visited the woman in ward 47.

	Ward 39	Ward 47	Ward 53	Doherty	Ledsham	Saxenby	No. 26	No. 65	No. 81
Mr. Cropper									
Mrs. Downes									
Mrs. Fell									
No. 26									
No. 65									
No. 81									
Doherty									
Ledsham									
Saxenby									

Patient	Ward	Visitor	House number

Fast away

INDIAN FILE

Four friends went out for a walk along the river bank, and at one point were obliged by the narrowness of the path, and the vegetation, to proceed in single file, as shown in the diagram. From the clues given below, can you fully identify walkers 1 to 4, and say what each does for a living?

1 Miss Mills works as a clerk in the offices of the local council.

2 Bridget is walking directly behind the dental receptionist as they go in single file along the path.

3 Miss Sanders is following immediately behind Annette.

4 Position 1 is occupied by the librarian, who is not Carla.

5 Diana, who is the teacher, is not in position 2 in the file, and her surname is not Langton.

First names: Annette; Bridget; Carla; Diana
Surnames: Brett; Langton; Mills; Sanders
Jobs: Council clerk; dental receptionist; librarian; teacher

First name: _____ _____ _____ _____

Surname: _____ _____ _____ _____

Job: _____ _____ _____ _____

Starting tip: Begin by working out what Bridget does for a living.

3 BRIDES FOR 3 BROTHERS

Three brothers recently married, each at the home church of his bride. From the clues given below, can you name each brother's bride and say where each couple were married?

1 The pair married at Holy Trinity included neither Rodney nor Diana, who did not marry each other.
2 William married Miss Belfry.
3 June's wedding took place at St John's.
4 Megan's new husband was not Shaun, whose wife's maiden name was not Hiles.

	Diana	June	Megan	Belfry	Hiles	Pugh	All Saints	Holy Trinity	St John's
Rodney									
Shaun									
William									
All Saints									
Holy Trinity									
St John's									
Belfry									
Hiles									
Pugh									

Husband	Bride	Maiden name	Church

the old year passes,

AWAY DAYS

Each year people are going further afield for their Christmas breaks. From the clues given below, can you work out the destinations, lengths of stay, and house numbers of three residents of Cedar Grove, Stocktown?

1 The Appletons live next door to the couple who went to Paris; the latter family's holiday was shorter than that of the former.

2 The Plumbs had their Christmas break in London.

3 The couple from No. 9 were away for five days.

4 The Cranstons live at No. 13.

	No. 9	No. 11	No. 13	London	Paris	Rome	Four days	Five days	Six days
Appleton									
Cranston									
Plumb									
Four days									
Five days									
Six days									
London									
Paris									
Rome									

Name	House no.	Destination	Duration

DOWN IN THE WOODS

In the new horror movie *Darkwood*, a group of seven movie students set out to make a documentary about the disappearance of another, similar party in a remote New England forest ten years before. In the first four days, four of the party die, leaving the other three, including the usual two gorgeous blondes, to try to save themselves. Yes, it's just about the sort of garbage you'd expect, but still, from the clues given here, can you work out the names and roles in the group of the four students who disappear, the days on which they are killed, and what kills them?

1 Zack Young, who dies on Monday, the first of the party to be lost, isn't the party's cook, who gets his comeuppance at the hands or, rather, the fangs of a vampire.

2 It's the group's sound recordist who is killed on Thursday.

3 Chip Brennan is slaughtered by zombies the day after one of his companions falls victim to a werewolf.

4 Thad Sorino, the party's local guide, isn't the person slain by the sasquatch or "bigfoot."

	Cameraman	Cook	Guide	Sound recordist	Monday	Tuesday	Wednesday	Thursday	Sasquatch	Vampire	Werewolf	Zombies
Chip Brennan												
Jake Keppler												
Thad Sorino												
Zack Young												
Sasquatch												
Vampire												
Werewolf												
Zombies												
Monday												
Tuesday												
Wednesday												
Thursday												

Name	Role	Day	Cause

Fa la la la la.

SUKO

Enter the numbers 1 to 9 in the spaces so that the number in each circle is equal to the sum of its four surrounding squares. Each colored area should add up to the color totals below.

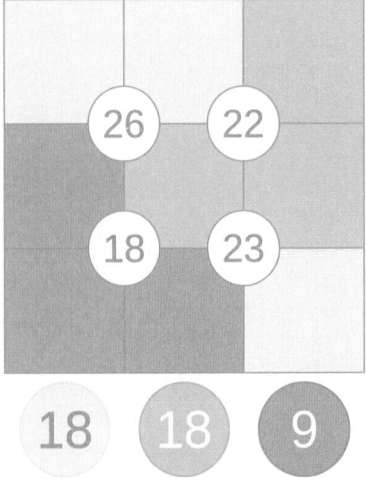

TROPHIES

Karen Mills is 17, and a talented athlete. On the mantelpiece of her parents' home are displayed the three trophies she's won this year. From the clues below, can you fill in on the diagram the details of each trophy: her placing, the event, the competition, and the month?

1 The 1,500 meters trophy was won the month after she received the third-place award, which isn't trophy A.

2 Her discus trophy stands to the left of the one she won in July.

3 Trophy B was won at the State Amateur Athletics Association meeting, for a placing one higher than she achieved in the high jump.

4 It was in the annual town sports that she took a first place.

Placings: First; second; third
Events: Discus; 1,500 meters; high jump
Meetings: State; inter-schools; town
Months: May; June; July

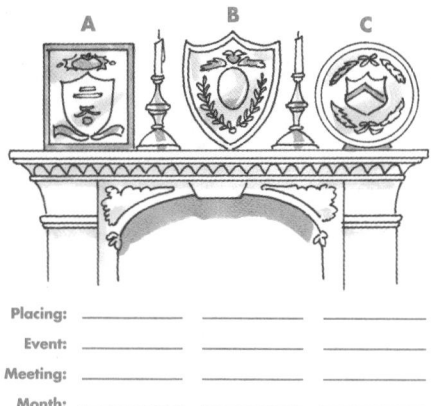

	A	B	C
Placing:	_____	_____	_____
Event:	_____	_____	_____
Meeting:	_____	_____	_____
Month:	_____	_____	_____

Starting tip: Work out for which place Trophy B was awarded.

la la la la la.

HAPPY FAMILIES

Three married couples who live near each other have different numbers of children. From the clues given below, can you match husbands and wives, and work out each couple's surname, and the number of children they have?

1 Bill and his wife have fewer children than the Bells.
2 Alan has more children than Judy.
3 Deborah Vickers is not the wife of Rick.
4 Meg is the mother of three; her surname is not Pearson.

	Deborah	Judy	Meg	Bell	Pearson	Vickers	Two	Three	Four
Alan									
Bill									
Rick									
Two									
Three									
Four									
Bell									
Pearson									
Vickers									

Husband	Wife	Surname	Children

DRESSING DOWN

Last Friday was a "dressing down day" at the Head Office of Chalke and Cheyse (Electronics) Inc, with all the employees being encouraged to come to work in casual clothing. Even so, everyone thought that four of the managers had rather overdone it—until they discovered that there was a wager made between them to see who could look the most outrageous. From the clues given below, can you work out which department each manager heads, and what type of upper and lower garments he or she wore last Friday?

1 The HR manager, who wore bright red ski pants on Friday, isn't Margaret Porter.

2 Bruce White is in charge of Research; the Accounts manager turned up on "dressing down day" in a frilly-fronted dress shirt.

3 Nigel Cook, who wore a kilt on Friday, is not the Accounts manager and was not the person in the sweater.

4 One of the managers turned up in a Rolling Stones T-shirt and a pair of filthy old shorts that must have normally been kept for gardening wear.

	Accounts	HR	Research	Sales	Beach shirt	Dress shirt	T-shirt	Sweater	Jeans	Kilt	Shorts	Ski pants
Mr. Cook												
Mrs. James												
Ms. Porter												
Mr. White												
Jeans												
Kilt												
Shorts												
Ski pants												
Beach shirt												
Dress shirt												
T-shirt												
Sweater												

Name	Department	Upper garment	Lower garment

Hail the new,

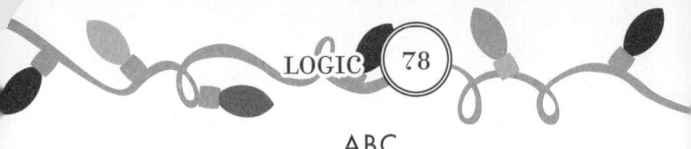

ABC

Each line, across and down, is to have each of the letters A, B, C, and D, and two empty squares. The letter outside the grid shows the first or second letter in the direction of the arrow. Can you fill in the grid?

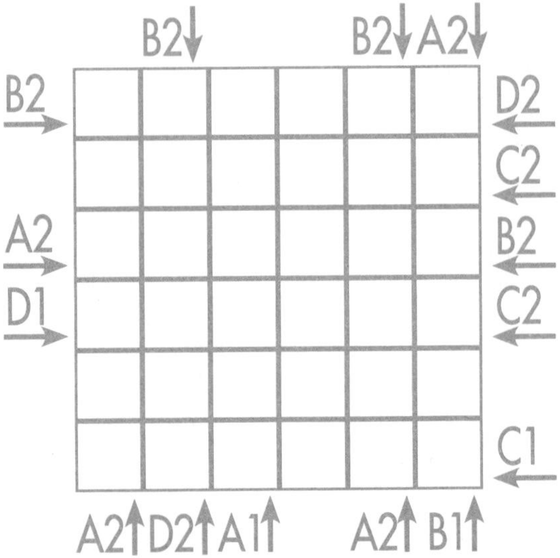

	B2↓			B2↓	A2↓	
B2→						D2←
						C2←
A2→						B2←
D1→						C2←
						C1←
	A2↑	D2↑ A1↑		A2↑	B1↑	

REQUEST STOP

The four people standing at the bus stop, numbered 1 to 4 in the diagram, are all waiting for different buses. From the clues given below, can you identify the four, and work out the number of the bus each will catch?

1 Mark's bus has a single-digit number; he is immediately behind the passenger named Parkes.

2 Harry is two places ahead of Simon Jubb in the queue.

3 The number 18 bus will be caught by passenger 3, who is not Jack.

4 The number 7 bus is awaited by the passenger named Newell.

5 The person at the head of the queue is not waiting for a number 12 bus.

First names: Harry; Jack; Mark; Simon
Surnames: Archer; Jubb; Newell; Parkes
Buses: 3; 7; 12; 18

First name: _____ _____ _____ _____

Surname: _____ _____ _____ _____

Bus: _____ _____ _____ _____

Starting tip: Begin by working out the first name of passenger 3.

ye lads and lasses,

BEHIND THE TIMES

My elderly friend Alice used a taxicab three times last week and on every occasion it was late. From the clues given, can you work out what time she ordered it for each day, how many minutes late it was, and where she was due to go?

1 The cab was less than 15 minutes late when it was ordered for 9:20; this was later in the week than when it was ordered for 11:15.

2 It was on Thursday that Alice went to her chiropractor's and did not have to wait 10 minutes for the cab.

3 The cab was only 5 minutes late for her trip to the garden center.

4 On the day when she had a hospital appointment, which was not Friday, she ordered the cab for 2:40.

	9:20	11:15	2:40	5 mins	10 mins	15 mins	Chiropodist	Garden center	Hospital
Tuesday									
Thursday									
Friday									
Chiropodist									
Garden center									
Hospital									
5 mins									
10 mins									
15 mins									

Day	Time required	Minutes late	Destination

WRITING STYLE

Three authors have got new books just published. From the given clues, work out the name of each author's book, their genre, and how many publications they have had.

1 Holden A. Gunn is the seasoned crime writer. He did not write *Winter Sun*.

2 *Diamond in the Rough* is the first novel by an exciting young writer, but it is not about gardening.

3 Rose Budd is the gardener, but has not published twenty books.

	1st	3rd	20th	Diamond in the Rough	Paradise Green	Winter Sun	Crime	Gardening	Romance
Holden A. Gunn									
Fleur Honeysuckle									
Rose Budd									
Crime						
Gardening						
Romance						
Diamond in the Rough			
Paradise Green			
Winter Sun			

Author	Title	Genre	Book no.

Fa la la la la,

SUKO

Enter the numbers 1 to 9 in the spaces so that the number in each circle is equal to the sum of its four surrounding squares. Each colored area should add up to the color totals below.

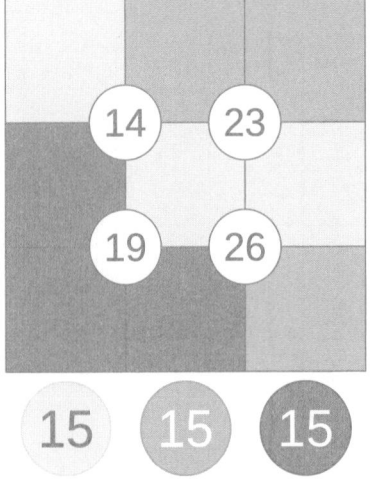

BAKE ME A CAKE

The cake stall is always popular at the monthly church fund-raising event. This month the four cakes at the front of the stall, numbered 1 to 4 in the diagram, were sold within seconds of the opening. From the clues given below, can you describe each cake, and name the woman who made it and the one who bought it?

1 Thelma bought the cake made by Mary, which was immediately to the right of the chocolate cake on the table.

2 Betty did not make the carrot cake, which was not bought by Linda, and Jean's cake was not number 4.

3 Cake 2 was made by Eileen.

4 The ginger sponge cake was in position 3 on the stall.

5 The lemon sponge was next but one on the table to the cake bought by Hilary.

Cakes: Chocolate; ginger sponge; carrot cake; lemon sponge
Cake bakers: Betty; Eileen; Jean; Mary
Buyers: Hilary; Linda; Sarah; Thelma

	1	2	3	4
Cake:	_____	_____	_____	_____
Made by:	_____	_____	_____	_____
Bought by:	_____	_____	_____	_____

Starting tip: Start by numbering the chocolate cake.

la la la la.

ENJOYING A TREAT

Three friends each treated themselves on different days last week. From the clues given, can you identify the three, and say what form their treat took, and on which day they enjoyed it?

1 Appropriately, it was Mrs. Feast who treated herself to a meal in an expensive restaurant.

2 Penelope enjoyed her treat the day after the woman who bought a new dress.

3 It was on Wednesday that one friend treated herself to an expensive new hairdo.

4 Ariadne is not Mrs. Junkett, who treated herself earlier in the week.

	Feast	Junkett	Revell	Expensive hairdo	Meal out	New dress	Wednesday	Thursday	Friday
Ariadne									
Daphne									
Penelope									
Wednesday									
Thursday									
Friday									
Expensive hairdo									
Meal out									
New dress									

First name	Surname	Treat	Day

FIRST CITIZENS

Northchester City Council have just taken delivery of portraits of four previous mayors of the city, which are to be hung in the town hall. From the clues below, can you work out the name of each of the four mayors pictured, the name of the artist, the medium in which the portrait has been executed, and where in the town hall it will be exhibited?

1 The portrait of Jack Morris is the work of David Bell.

2 The portrait of William Moody is not the watercolor.

3 The charcoal sketch of Alfred Chinn is neither the portrait by Beryl Hunt nor the Peter Nash picture that is to be hung in the town clerk's office.

4 The picture of Percy Norman is the work of a female artist.

5 The oil painting that is to hang in the council chamber depicts a mayor with a longer name than the one whose portrait will be on show in the mayor's office.

	Beryl Hunt	David Bell	Peter Nash	Susan Webb	Acrylic painting	Charcoal sketch	Oil painting	Watercolor painting	Council chamber	Entrance hall	Mayor's office	Town clerk's office
Alfred Chinn												
Jack Morris												
Percy Norman												
William Moody												
Council chamber												
Entrance hall												
Mayor's office												
Town clerk's office												
Acrylic painting												
Charcoal sketch												
Oil painting												
Watercolor painting												

Major	Artist	Painting medium	Hung in

Sing we joyous,

ABC

Each line, across and down, is to have each of the letters A, B, C, and D, and two empty squares. The letter outside the grid shows the first or second letter in the direction of the arrow. Can you fill in the grid?

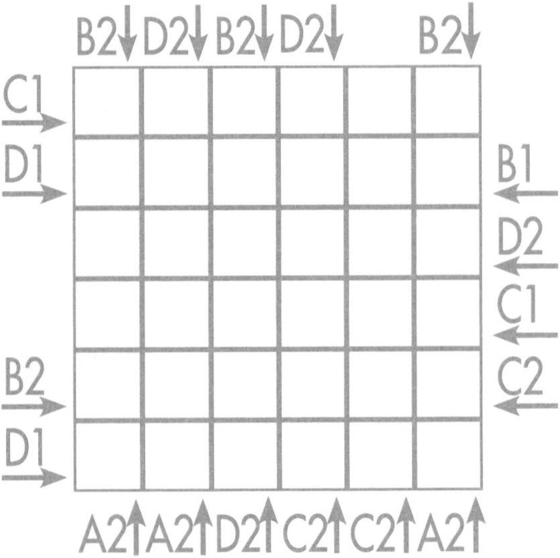

B2↓ D2↓ B2↓ D2↓   B2↓

C1→

D1→   B1←

                      D2←

                      C1←

B2→   C2←

D1→

A2↑ A2↑ D2↑ C2↑ C2↑ A2↑

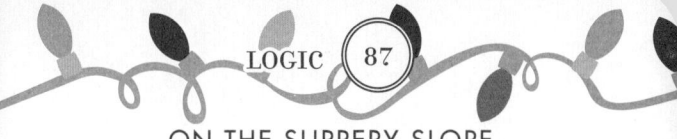

ON THE SLIPPERY SLOPE

It was the height of the winter sports season, and four celebrities were skiing on an exclusive Squaw Valley piste, in the positions numbered 1 to 4 in the diagram. From the clues given below, can you fully identify and describe each of the four skiers?

1 Julius Benson was somewhere behind the media mogul as they descended the piste.

2 Watson is number 4 in the diagram.

3 No two skiers had an identical set of initials.

4 Miranda is the off-duty senator, and Max is skier number 2.

5 Winsford is the movie star's surname.

First names: Davina; Julius; Max; Miranda
Surnames: Benson; Levitt; Watson; Winsford
Descriptions: Airline owner; senator; movie star; media mogul

First name: _____ _____ _____ _____
Surname: _____ _____ _____ _____
Description: _____ _____ _____ _____

Starting tip: Begin by working out what Julius Benson is.

all together,

ANIMAL POP-UPS

Paul has a toy that is a long box with four compartments, each in different colored plastic, the tops of which, when a button is pressed, pop up to reveal a different animal picture. From the clues given below, can you work out the color of compartments 1 to 4, say which animal each conceals, and say in which order Paul pressed the buttons to make them appear when he last played with this toy?

1 Paul pressed the blue button immediately after the one that produces the tiger.

2 The elephant appears on the lid of compartment 1, which is not green.

3 The last compartment lid to pop up was number 3, but button 4 was not pressed first.

4 The lion was the second animal Paul revealed.

5 The camel is on the lid of the red compartment.

Colors: Blue; green; red; yellow
Animals: Camel; elephant; lion; tiger
Order: First; second; third; fourth

Animal:	_____	_____	_____	_____
Color:	_____	_____	_____	_____
Order:	_____	_____	_____	_____

Starting tip: Start by working out which animal is depicted on the lid of compartment 3.

DUTY DRESSES

After a minor operation, Alice has been visited at home on three successive days by community nurses from her local care center in order to change the dressing and make sure everything is OK. From the clues given below, can you work out their full names and the days and times of their visits?

1 Nurse Williams dressed Alice's wound the day after Sharon.

2 The Tuesday visit was at 10:30.

3 Nurse Hodgson called on Thursday; her first name is not Carolyn.

4 Jane's visit was not at 10:00.

	Hodgson	Lowry	Williams	Tuesday	Wednesday	Thursday	9:30	10:00	10:30
Carolyn									
Jane									
Sharon									
9:30									
10:00									
10:30									
Tuesday									
Wednesday									
Thursday									

First name	Surname	Day	Time

Fa la la,

FIRM FRIENDS

Three women have been taken on by a firm during the last year. From the clues given below, can you identify the three, work out each woman's role in the firm, and say exactly how long each has been employed there?

1 Maxine has been with the firm longer than the computer operator.

2 The most recent employee to join the firm's staff is Mrs. Oxley.

3 The manager's personal assistant, Ms. Buller, has not worked for the firm as long as Carol.

	Buller	Coward	Oxley	Computer operator	Manager's PA	Receptionist	Four months	Seven months	Ten months
Carol									
Maxine									
Sheila									
4 months									
7 months									
10 months									
Computer operator									
Manager's PA									
Receptionist									

First name	Surname	Role	Time

JOINT CONCERNS

Three men sat in the waiting room of the Orthopedic Clinic. From the clues given below, can you work out each man's full name, the time of his appointment, and which of his joints had caused problems?

1 The man whose ankle was mending after a break had the 2:20 appointment.
2 Robert's appointment was not 2:40.
3 John, whose surname is not Milton, had had a knee operation.
4 Mr. Jonson's time was next before that of the man who had had a hip replacement.

	Burns	Jonson	Milton	2:00	2:20	2:40	Ankle	Hip	Knee
Ben									
John									
Robert									
Ankle									
Hip									
Knee									
2:00									
2:20									
2:40									

First name	Surname	Time	Joint

la la la,

SUKO

Enter the numbers 1 to 9 in the spaces so that the number in each circle is equal to the sum of its four surrounding squares. Each colored area should add up to the color totals below.

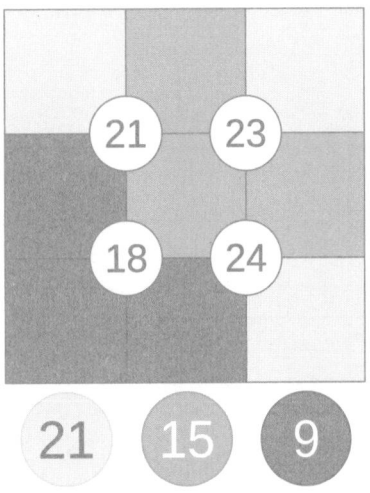

BEHIND CLOSED DOORS

The diagram shows four study doors in the corridor of a university building, each belonging to one of the academic staff in the same department. From the clues given below, can you fully identify the occupant of the room behind each door, and name his or her role in the department?

1 The head of the department is Professor Spriggs.

2 The door of the man named Darby is adjacent to Melissa's.

3 The person who uses study D is senior in the department to Arabella, but is the junior of Chubb, whose door is not the one marked A.

4 The junior lecturer's door is somewhere to the right of Graham's.

First names: Arabella; Graham; Jolyon; Melissa
Surnames: Chubb; Darby; Howlett; Spriggs
Positions (in ascending order of seniority):
Junior lecturer; lecturer; senior lecturer; professor

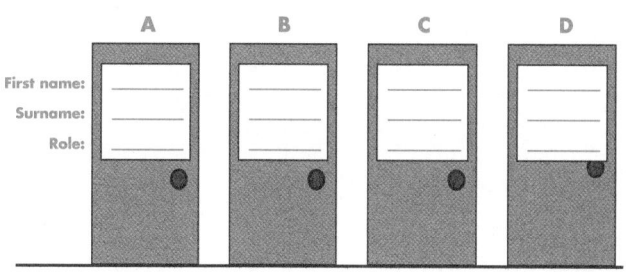

	A	B	C	D
First name:				
Surname:				
Role:				

Starting tip: Begin by working out Chubb's role in the department.

la la la.

RISING STARS

Three budding young actors have just got their first breaks in showbiz. From the given clues, work out in which city each of them is working and in what medium and genre they are starring.

1 The movie telling the history of the Pilgrim Fathers has an unheard of leading lady. It is being filmed in the United States.
2 Liona Couch is treading the boards for the first time in an old theater, but not in London.
3 Justin Spotlight's comic timing landed him his new role.
4 Constance Hamm is not in New York.

	Los Angeles	London	New York	Movie	Stage	TV	Comedy	History	Tragedy
Constance Hamm									
Justin Spotlight									
Liona Couch									
Comedy									
History									
Tragedy									
Movie									
Stage									
TV									

Actor	City	Medium	Genre

NONSTEREOTYPICAL

On the evening of St. Patrick's Day, four Irish friends all now based in New York were having a celebratory drink in the Green Man bar when one of them observed that—with one honorable exception—none of them fitted the usual employment stereotypes associated with their countrymen. From the clues given below, can you work out each man's full name, which Irish county he was born in, and his present occupation?

1 The award-winning journalist surnamed Byrne has a first name two letters shorter than that of the man from County Wexford.

2 O'Sullivan, who hails from a little village in County Limerick, is not the Roman Catholic priest.

3 Barry's surname isn't O'Kelly, and Sean doesn't come from County Clare.

4 The lawyer was born in County Galway.

5 Declan isn't the neurosurgeon.

	Byrne	MacFeeter	O'Kelly	O'Sullivan	Clare	Galway	Limerick	Wexford	Lawyer	Journalist	Neurosurgeon	Priest
Barry												
Declan												
Pat												
Sean												
Lawyer												
Journalist												
Neurosurgeon												
Priest												
Clare												
Galway												
Limerick												
Wexford												

First name	Surname	County	Profession

Heedless of the wind

ABC

Each line, across and down, is to have each of the letters A, B, C, and D, and two empty squares. The letter outside the grid shows the first or second letter in the direction of the arrow. Can you fill in the grid?

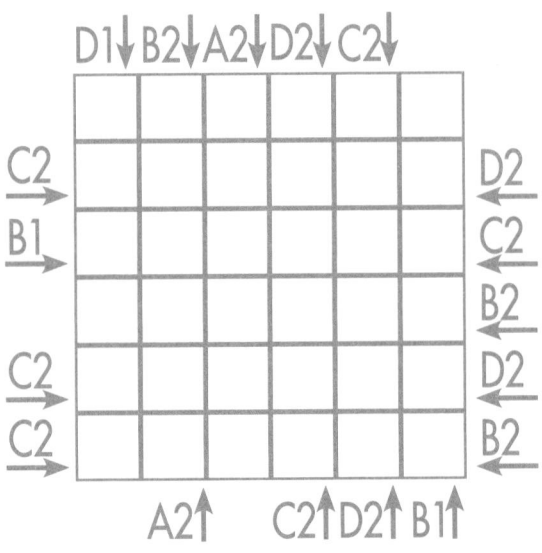

TRICK OR TREAT

Last Halloween, four friends, dressed in various disguises, went knocking on doors in Lilac Drive. From the clues given below, can you work out, at the moment encapsulated in the diagram, the full identity of the girl knocking at each door, and describe the disguise she was wearing?

1 Pamela, disguised as a witch, was knocking at a door on the same side of the street as the girl named Cantrip.

2 The snake-girl, who was not Caroline, was at a higher-numbered house than the dragon-girl.

3 The goblin was offering a "trick or treat" to the owner of No. 5.

4 No. 8 Lilac Drive was being visited by Miss Fowles.

5 Delia was calling at No. 17; her surname is not Knight.

First names: Caroline; Delia; Lesley; Pamela
Surnames: Baynes; Cantrip; Fowles; Knight
Disguises: Dragon; goblin; snake; witch

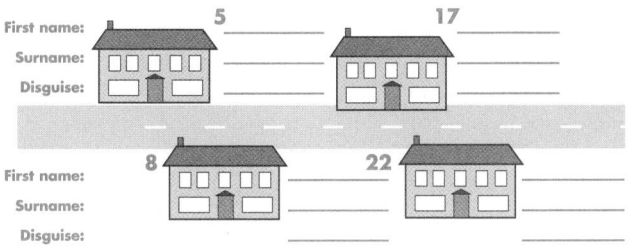

First name: **5** _____ **17** _____
Surname: _____ _____
Disguise: _____ _____

First name: **8** _____ **22** _____
Surname: _____ _____
Disguise: _____ _____

Starting tip: First work out the number of which Miss Cantrip is calling.

and weather,

MORNING PAPERS

The newspaper kiosk at Raylweigh Station has seven newspapers displayed on its counter. From the clues given below, can you fill in on the diagram the name of each paper displayed?

1. The *Daily Gazette* is next to, and on the same row as, a paper with a one-word name.
2. Newspaper 1, which doesn't have the word *Daily* in its title, isn't the *Bulletin*.
3. The *Monitor* is immediately right of, and on the same row as, the *Daily Journal*.
4. The *Daily Mercury* is displayed between, and on the same row as, the *Pictorial* and the *Daily Review*.

Newspaper names: *Bulletin; Daily Gazette; Daily Journal; Daily Mercury; Daily Review; Monitor; Pictorial*

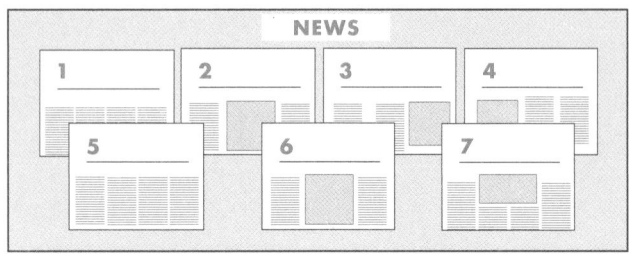

Starting tip: Work out the title of newspaper 1.

SKI TRIP

Three friends who each pursue a different sport each ended up breaking a different part of their anatomy after an accident while enjoying their favorite pastime. From the clues given below, can you say who broke what while indulging in which activity in which month of the year?

1 The skiing accident took place in January.

2 Glyn broke his collarbone, but not while hang gliding.

3 The February accident resulted in a broken arm, which was not the injury sustained by Will.

4 The leg was not broken in March.

	Arm	Collarbone	Leg	Hang gliding	Motocross	Skiing	January	February	March
Glyn									
Jerry									
Will									
January									
February									
March									
Hang gliding						
Motocross						
Skiing						

Name	Injury	Activity	Month

Fa la la la la, la la la la

CHRISTMAS CALLS

On Christmas Day we received four phone calls from friends whose jobs had taken them to distant parts of the globe. From the clues given below, can you work out who rang when, what their job is, and where they rang from?

1 The doctor rang an hour after Pete, who phoned from Kingston, Jamaica.

2 The midday call came from Dakar, Senegal.

3 Mike is a teacher employed to work abroad.

4 Vikki was the earliest of the four callers.

5 Anna's call was separated by more than an hour from the one from New Zealand, which wasn't from the Army officer.

	Anna	Mike	Pete	Vikki	Doctor	Journalist	Army officer	Teacher	Jamaica	Kuwait	New Zealand	Senegal
10:00 a.m.												
11:00 a.m.												
12 noon												
1:00 p.m.												
Jamaica												
Kuwait												
New Zealand												
Senegal												
Doctor												
Journalist												
Army officer												
Teacher												

Time	Name	Occupation	Location

pocket posh®
christmas logic 5
SOLUTIONS

SOLUTIONS

1 The woman from No.13 is to entertain her sister (clue 1), so she cannot be May, who is to have her daughter Susan (clue 2) or Lill, who is to have her cousin (clue 3), so must be Elsa. Therefore, David must be a guest at No.15 (clue 4). Since Lill's house is not No.13, the one where Roger is to stay cannot be No.11 (clue 3), so must be No.13. He cannot therefore be Susan's husband nor is the latter Christopher (clue 2), so Susan's husband must be David. Therefore, with May living at No. 15, Lill's house must be No.11. Her guest is not Jane (clue 5), so must be Wendy, whose husband, by elimination, must be Christopher. Jane must therefore be Elsa's sister and Roger must be her husband.

Thus:
Elsa, No.13, Jane and Roger.
May, No.15, Susan and David.
Lill, No.11, Wendy and Christopher.

2 Mr. Andrews was fined $2 (clue 1) and Arthur was fined $1 (clue 3), so Charlie Chaplin (clue 4) must have been fined $1.50. By elimination, Brian must have been fined $2 and is therefore Mr. Andrews, and Arthur must be Mr. Brown. He was not returning a book (clue 1) and Brian was returning the DVD, so Arthur Brown must have borrowed the CD. By elimination, Charlie Chaplin must have borrowed the book.

Thus:
Arthur Brown, CD, $1.
Brian Andrews, DVD, $2.
Charlie Chaplin, book, $1.50.

3 Alistair is 9 (clue 4). The oldest child, who produced picture 1 (clue 2), cannot be Mary (clue 1), or Silas, whose monocled character is somewhere to the right of another (clue 3), so she must be Jennifer. We now know Silas is not 9 or 11, nor is he 8 (clue 3), so he must be 10, leaving Mary as 8. So, from clue 1, picture 2 must have been drawn by Alistair, aged 9. This face is clean-shaven (clue 1), but does not have the monocle, so it must be wearing spectacles. From clue 3, Mary must have drawn picture 3, and Silas picture 4. From clue 4, picture 1 does not have a mustache, so it must have a beard, leaving the mustache adorning picture 3.

Thus:
1, Jennifer, 11, beard.
2, Alistair, 9, spectacles.
3, Mary, 8, mustache.
4, Silas, 10, monocle.

4

2	8	6
1	4	5
9	3	7

(15) (23) (17) (19)

5 Saul and his companion ate at the Golden Goose (clue 3), so Harry and Kitty, who did not eat at the Taj Mahal (clue 1), must have favored the Phoenix. So they did not eat out on Monday (clue 1), or Friday (clue 2), and must have done so on Wednesday. So, from clue 1, the Taj Mahal was visited on Monday, and, by elimination, the man who ate there must have been Magnus. Also by elimination, Saul must have eaten at the Golden Goose on Friday. His companion there must have been Lucinda (clue 2), leaving Pearl as the companion of Magnus at the Taj Mahal.

Thus:

Harry, Kitty, Phoenix, Wednesday.
Magnus, Pearl, Taj Mahal, Monday.
Saul, Lucinda, Golden Goose, Friday.

6 Richfield are Rowdies (clue 2), so Middleby, who are not the Eagles (clue 3), must be Kickers, leaving the Eagles as Lockstead. Lester is Cross (clue 2), so Evan, who is not Pass (clue 1), must be Trapp, leaving Delroy as Pass. So Evan must play for Middleby Kickers (clue 3). Lester Cross is not with Richfield Rowdies (clue 2), so he must be a Lockstead Eagles trainee, leaving Delroy Pass on the books of Richfield Rowdies.

Thus:

Delroy Pass, Richfield Rowdies.
Evan Trapp, Middleby Kickers.
Lester Cross, Lockstead Eagles.

7 Pistols Crocetti in cell 4 (clue 3) can't be the numbers racketeer (clue 2), who also can't be Wolf Levitch from Atlantic City (clue 2). Duke Fitzgerald ran the protection racket (clue 1), so the numbers racketeer must be Rosy Schwartz. We now know the city or the crime for three convicts, so the bootlegger from Boston (clue 4) must be Pistols Crocetti in cell 4, and, by elimination, Wolf Levitch from Atlantic City must have been jailed for bank robbery. Since he isn't in cell 4, numbers racketeer Rosy Schwartz can't be in cell 3 (clue 2), nor is he in cell 2 (clue 3), so he must be in cell 1, and, from clue 2, Wolf Levitch must be in cell 2. By elimination, Duke Fitzgerald must be in cell 3; he's not from New York (clue 1), so must be from Chicago, and the New Yorker must be Rosy Schwartz in cell 1.

Thus:

Cell 1, Rosy Schwartz, New York, numbers racket.
Cell 2, Wolf Levitch, Atlantic City, bank robbery.
Cell 3, Duke Fitzgerald, Chicago, protection racket.
Cell 4, Pistols Crocetti, Boston, bootlegger.

8 Miranda is in caravan 3 (clue 4), so the woman in caravan 4, who cannot be Alicia from Chicago (clue 1), or Zoe, the companion of Sebastian (clue 3), must be Esme. Therefore, from clue 2, Miranda, in caravan 3, is from Boston, and Desmond is in caravan 2. So Sebastian and Zoe, whose caravan we know is not 3 or 4, must be in caravan 1, and, by elimination, Alicia from Chigago must be sharing caravan 2 with Desmond. Sebastian and Zoe are not from L.A. (clue 3), so they must be from El Paso, leaving L.A. as Esme's home city. Miranda's partner is not Luther (clue 4), so he must be Paul, leaving Esme with Luther.

Thus:

  1, Sebastian and Zoe, El Paso.
  2, Desmond and Alicia, Chicago.
  3, Paul and Miranda, Boston.
  4, Luther and Esme, Los Angeles.

9 Bernstein, who won the race, is not Karl (clue 3), nor can he be Gus (clue 2), so he must be Chris. Potter was not third (clue 4), so he must have been second, leaving third place for Lopez, whose car was the Tarantula (clue 1). The Cougar was not second (clue 4), so it must have been Chris Bernstein's winning car, and the Rapide must have finished second. So, from clue 2, Gus must be Lopez, who finished third, leaving Karl as the second-placed driver, Potter.

Thus:

  First, Chris Bernstein, Cougar.
  Second, Karl Potter, Rapide.
  Third, Gus Lopez, Tarantula.

10

C		B		A	D
A		C	D	B	
	B	D	A		C
	D	A	C		B
B	C			D	A
D	A		B	C	

11 Allenby is trailing green smoke (clue 1), so Corporal Havelock, who is not trailing red smoke (clue 3) or blue (clue 4), must trail orange smoke. Figure C is the private (clue 2), so figure A, who can't be the captain (clue 1), and who is not corporal Havelock (clue 3), must be the sergeant. His surname can't be Wolfe (clue 4), nor is that the captain's name (clue 1), and we know it's not the corporal's, so it must be the private's. Allenby, trailing green smoke, can't be figure D (clue 1), nor, since the captain isn't figure C, can he be figure B (clue 1), so he must be figure A, the sergeant. Therefore, from clue 1, the captain must be figure B, and, by elimination, corporal Havelock must be figure D. From clue 4, the man trailing blue smoke must be surnamed Gordon, and, by elimination, he must be the captain, figure B. Finally, figure C, private Wolfe, must be trailing red smoke.

Thus:

A, Sergeant Allenby, green.
B, Captain Gordon, blue.
C, Private Wolfe, red.
D, Corporal Havelock, orange.

12 Mike's longest word was MANNER so George, who did not make GAILY (clue 1) must have made DREADED and John's, GAILY. John's total was 182 (clue 4), so Mike's, which was not 176 (clue 2), must have been 169 and George's, therefore, 176. George's best score was 18 (clue 1), so Mike, whose total of 169 means that his best score was not 24 (clue 3), must have had a best score of 36, leaving John's as 24.

Thus:

George, DREADED, 18 points, 176.
John, GAILY, 24 points, 182.
Mike, MANNER, 36 points, 169.

13 John is a teacher (clue 1), so the bank manager living in Davenport, who is not Samuel (clue 3), must be Charles, who was born in Glenwood (clue 2), and, by elimination, Samuel must be the lawyer. He was not born in Vinton (clue 3), so he must have been born in Sioux City, leaving John as the brother born in Vinton. Finally, from clue 4, Samuel does not live in Ames, so he must live in Waterloo, leaving Ames as John's place of residence. In summary:
Charles, Glenwood, bank manager, Davenport.
John, Vinton, teacher, Ames.
Samuel, Sioux City, lawyer, Waterloo.

14

2		6		5
	12		23	
1		3		9
	19		24	
7		8		4

15 The 2010 hotel was the Pavilion (clue 2) and the 2013 fancy dress theme was Gangsters (clue 4), so in 2012, when the NLA didn't use the Undercliff Hotel in Longsands (clue 1), or the Metropole (clue 3), they must have booked the Grand. Therefore the Southbay resort where the ball theme was Beach Party must have been booked in 2010 (clue 5). From clue 3, the Wild West–themed ball can't have been in 2011, so it must have been in 2012, at the Grand, and in 2011 the hotel must have been the Metropole. By elimination, the convention at the Undercliff, Longsands (clue 1) must have been held in 2013 with the Gangsters fancy dress theme, and the Super Heroes theme must have been used at the Metropole in 2011. This wasn't in Wairmouth, so must have been in Brightbourne, leaving Wairmouth as the resort where the 2012 convention was held at the Grand Hotel.

Thus:

2010, Pavilion, Southbay, Beach Party.
2011, Metropole, Brightbourne, Super Heroes.
2012, Grand, Wairmouth, Wild West.
2013, Undercliff, Longsands, Gangsters.

16 David is not Fox (clue 1), nor can he be Coney, in position 1 (clues 1 and 3). Kevin is Mole (clue 4), so David's surname must be Badger. Coney, in position 1, is not Joseph (clue 4), so he must be Richard, leaving Joseph as Fox. Since Kevin Mole is not in position 1, Joseph Fox cannot be in position 2 (clue 4), nor can he be in position 4 (clue 1), so he must be in position 3. So, from clue 1, David Badger must be in position 4, leaving Kevin Mole in position 2. Richard Coney's estimate cannot have been $150 (clue 3), nor were those of David or Joseph (clue 1), so that must have been Kevin's guess. $199 does not appear in front of players 1 or 4 (clue 2), so that must have been Joseph Fox's estimate. David did not guess $178 (clue 5), so he must have gone for $165, leaving $178 as Richard's estimate.

Thus:

1, Richard Coney, $178.
2, Kevin Mole, $150.
3, Joseph Fox, $199.
4, David Badger, $165.

17 The movie on at Studio A was *Return of the Ghouls* (clue 4), so *The Haunting*, which was not the movie at C (clue 1), must have been the one at B and *Nightmare* must have been at C. It was not seen by Mac Arborough (clue 3), or by Willy Dye, who saw *The Haunting* (clue 2), so must have been seen by Harry Kirry. Mac Arborough must therefore have seen *Return of the Ghouls*. He did not attend the 8:00 performance (clue 4) nor could Willy Dye have done (clue 1), so Harry Kirry must have chosen that time. Willy Dye also did not go for the 6:00 showing (clue 2), so must have preferred the 2:30 one, with Mac Arborough going for the 6:00 screening.

Thus:

Harry Kirry, *Nightmare*, Studio C, 8:00.
Mac Arborough, *Return of the Ghouls*, Studio A, 6:00.
Willy Dye, *The Haunting*, Studio B, 2:30.

18 Judith was with Paramount (clue 3), so Virginia Eidel, whose company was not Warner Brothers (clue 1), must have been the MGM starlet, leaving Hughie with Warner Brothers. So he was not 8 (clue 1), or 12 (clue 2), and must have been 10. Therefore, from clue 1, Virginia was 8, leaving Judith as the starlet aged 12. From clue 2, she must be Vedette, leaving Hughie's surname as Starr.

Thus:

Hughie Starr, 10, Warner Brothers.
Judith Vedette, 12, Paramount.
Virginia Eidel, 8, MGM.

19 Dawn's sandwiches didn't contain ham (clue 1), corned beef (clue 2), or cheese, which was eaten by a man (clue 4), so they must have contained salami. Amy Pigeon (clue 5) didn't have cheese sandwiches (clue 4), and we know she didn't have salami. Dawn, the salami-eater, isn't surnamed Bunting (clue 3), so the person who had ham sandwiches, whose surname is one letter shorter (clue 1), can't be Amy Pigeon, who must therefore have had corned beef. Therefore, from clue 2, Bill must have had the doughnut. Bunting's sandwiches didn't contain ham (clue 1) or salami (clue 3), so contained cheese, and Bunting's cake was therefore a cupcake (clue 4). He is male (clue 4), so, since Bill's cake was a doughnut, Bunting must be Colin and, by elimination, Bill must have had ham sandwiches. From clue 3, Dawn, who had salami sandwiches and didn't eat the chocolate cake, must have had a Danish pastry, and Amy Pigeon must have had the chocolate cake with her corned beef sandwiches. Finally, from clue 1, Bill must be Swan and Dawn must be Finch.

Thus:

Amy Pigeon, corned beef, chocolate cake.
Bill Swan, ham, doughnut.
Colin Bunting, cheese, cupcake.
Dawn Finch, salami, Danish pastry.

20

C			D	B	A
D	A	C	B		
B	C		A		D
	D	C	A	B	
	B	A		D	C
A	D	B		C	

21 Grant is in car 1 (clue 4), and Eleanor in car 2 (clue 5). One of the boys has car 3, which is yellow (clue 2), so Daphne Allen (clue 3) must be in car 4. We know the yellow car 3 is not driven by Grant or Allen, and clue 1 tells us Briggs is in the blue car, so it must be Powell who is driving car 3. Therefore, by elimina-tion, Eleanor's surname must be Briggs, and her car is therefore blue. So, from clue 1, Lewis must be Grant, at the wheel of car 1, leaving David as the boy in car 3. Daphne Allen's car is not red (clue 3), so it must be green, leaving Lewis Grant at the wheel of the red car.

Thus:

1, Lewis Grant, red.
2, Eleanor Briggs, blue.
3, David Powell, yellow.
4, Daphne Allen, green.

22 Sam is not the beagle (clue 1), and, as his owners are the Lead family (clue 1), he cannot be the chihuahua, who belongs to the Collers (clue 3). Max is the Yorkshire terrier (clue 6), so, by elimination, Sam must be the boxer. So he lives at No. 17 (clue 2). Therefore, from clue 1, the beagle must live at No. 19. So his owners are not called Kennell (clue 5). We know they are not Lead or Coller, so they must be called Bone. Now, by elimination, Max must belong to the Kennells. Since Freddie's home is No. 21 (clue 4), he cannot be the beagle, so he must be the Collers' chihuahua. By elimination, the beagle's name must be Dick, and the Kennells must live at No. 23.

Thus:

17, Lead, boxer, Sam.
19, Bone, beagle, Dick.
21, Coller, chihuahua, Freddie.
23, Kennell, Yorkshire terrier, Max.

23 Lorna's surname is Hilton (clue 4), so Anne, who is not Barley (clue 3), must be Lewis and Flora must be Barley. Anne Lewis goes for key lime pie (clue 1), so Lorna Hilton's favorite dessert, which is not apple pie (clue 4), must be ice cream and her favorite main course must therefore be jambalaya (clue 2). Anne does not care for crab cakes (clue 3), so her main choice must be fried chicken. By elimination, Flora must choose crab cakes followed by apple pie.

Thus:

Anne Lewis, fried chicken, key lime pie.

Flora Barley, crab cakes, apple pie.

Lorna Hilton, jambalaya, ice cream.

24

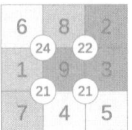

25 The laundress is female and so is the midwife (clue 5), so the doctor must have been male. So, from clue 1, Alfred Banks must have been the doctor and the publican, Henry Joad. The latter's dog was a greyhound (clue 2). The laundress's dog was a bulldog (clue 3), so Dr. Alfred Banks's dog, Diamond (clue 4), which wasn't a spaniel (clue 1), must have been a dalmatian. Now, from clue 6, Gladys Hope's dog must have been Traveler. It wasn't the spaniel, which from clue 1 must have been either Bounce or Midget, so it must have been the bulldog, and Gladys Hope was therefore the laundress. By elimination, Mary Newman must have been the midwife, and must have owned the spaniel. It wasn't called Bounce (clue 5), so must have been Midget, leaving Bounce as the greyhound owned by Henry Joad, the publican.

Thus:

Bounce, greyhound, Henry Joad, publican.

Diamond, Dalmatian, Alfred Banks, doctor.

Midget, spaniel, Mary Newman, midwife.

Traveler, bulldog, Gladys Hope, laundress.

26 Maxine went to Florida (clue 3). The couple who went to New York were not Janice and Ewan (clue 1), so the mother in question must have been Lucy, and, by elimination, Janice and Ewan must have spent their vacation in California. Their child is not Adam (clue 1), and Sally's father is Clyde (clue 2), so Denise must have visited California with Janice and Ewan. Maxine was not accompanied to Florida by Peter (clue 3), so her husband must be Clyde, and their child is therefore Sally, leaving Lucy's husband as Peter, and their child as Adam.

Thus:

> Janice, Ewan, Denise, California.
> Lucy, Peter, Adam, New York.
> Maxine, Clyde, Sally, Florida.

27 The person from Sheep Lane saw the yellow cube UFO (clue 4), the person from One Tree Hill saw the UFO over the reservoir (clue 5), and Eva Brick lives in Mill Street (clue 4), so the man who thought he saw a red triangle UFO over the hospital (clue 1) must live in Bush Grove. He isn't Alf Penny, who saw a UFO over the town hall (clue 3), so must be Sean Lamb. We now have a name or address for three places hovered over, so Eva Brick from Mill Street must have seen a UFO over the cemetery. So it wasn't the green disc (clue 2). Her address rules out the yellow cube and the position of her UFO, the red triangle, so she must have seen a white sphere.

By elimination, the person from Sheep Lane who saw the yellow cube must have been Alf Penny, and the cube therefore hovered over the town hall. Also by elimination the person on One Tree Hill who saw the UFO over the reservoir must have been Kitty Catt, who must have described it as a green disc.

Thus:

> Alf Penny, Sheep Lane, yellow cube, town hall.
> Eva Brick, Mill Street, white sphere, cemetery.
> Kitty Catt, One Tree Hill, green disc, reservoir.
> Sean Lamb, Bush Grove, red triangle, hospital.

28 The Hotel Splendide is at Lake Como (clue 2), so the Bella Vista, which is not at Lake Garda (clue 3), must be at Lake Maggiore and the Lake Garda hotel must be the Grand. So, from clue 1, David must have stayed at the Bella Vista. Rob did not stay at the Grand (clue 4), so his hotel must have been the Splendide and Tom must have gone to the Grand. Rob and Amanda are husband and wife (clue 4), so Claire's husband, who is not David (clue 1), must be Tom and David's wife must therefore be Kate.

Thus:

> David, Kate, Lake Maggiore, Bella Vista.
> Rob, Amanda, Lake Como, Spendide.
> Tom, Claire, Lake Garda, Grand.

29 Clue 3 shows that the two women cannot have sat opposite each other, so *Curse of the Mummy* must have been chosen by a man. He cannot have been Cranleigh Simister (clue 1), so must have been Dermot Goole. Clearly the two men also were not opposite, so *Bloodless Butchery* must have been a woman's choice. *Devil's Picnic* must have been a man's preference (clue 3), that of Simister, who must have sat opposite Gayle Plasmer (clue 3), so Deirdre Gore must be the woman who supported *Bloodless Butchery*. The clockwise sequence is therefore: Gore (*Bloodless Butchery*), Simister (*Devil's Picnic*), Goole (*Curse of the Mummy*), and Plasmer, who must have chosen *Fiend From Space*, and therefore sat at D (clue 4). So Gore must have been at A.

Thus:

A, Deirdre Gore, *Bloodless Butchery*.

B, Cranleigh Simister, *Devil's Picnic*.

C, Dermot Goole, *Curse of the Mummy*.

D, Gayle Plasmer, *Fiend From Space*.

30

C		D		B	A
A	D	B		C	
B	C		A	D	
D	A		B		C
		C	D	A	B
	B	A	C		D

31 Angie Bruce is on screen for 17 seconds (clue 3) and the actress playing the nurse is on screen for 47 seconds (clue 1), so Donna Essex, who appears as a cab driver for less than 54 seconds (clue 2), must be on screen for 29 seconds. We know that the nurse who's seen for 47 seconds isn't Angie Bruce or Donna Essex, nor can she be Julie Kirby (clue 1), so she must be Gail Hatton, and, from clue 1, Julie Kirby must be in *Plain Clothes*. By elimination, she must appear for 54 seconds. Therefore, from clue 2, Gail Hatton's 47 second appearance as a nurse must be in *Bad Company*. Angie Bruce's 17-second role isn't as an air hostess (clue 3), so must be as a receptionist, and the air hostess must be Julie Kirby. Finally, from clue 4, Angie Bruce's appearance isn't in *High Flyers*, so must be in *Green Sun*, and it's *High Flyers* in which Donna Essex appears for 29 seconds as a cab driver.

Thus:

Angie Bruce, 17 seconds, receptionist, *Green Sun*.
Donna Essex, 29 seconds, cab driver, *High Flyers*.
Gail Hatton, 47 seconds, nurse, *Bad Company*.
Julie Kirby, 54 seconds, air hostess, *Plain Clothes*.

32 The casino is in Blue Bay (clue 4), and the Barratts stayed in the town with the pleasure beach (clue 2). The Rhodes family stayed in Kingsville, which is not the location of the marina (clue 1), so it must be the town with the scuba diving center. We now know the family staying in Blue Bay, with its casino, were not the Barratts or the Rhodes, nor were they the Wardles (clue 4), so they must have been the Lesters, and Blue Bay is therefore resort B (clue 2). Resort D is Whitesands (clue 3). Kingsville, which is next clockwise round the coast from the marina resort (clue 1), cannot be resort C, so it must be resort A, leaving resort C as Nelson. The marina must be in Whitesands (clue 1), and, by elimination, it must have been the Wardles who were staying there. This leaves the pleasure beach in Nelson, so that must be where the Barratts spent their vacation.

Thus:

A, Kingsville, Rhodes, scuba diving center.
B, Blue Bay, Lester, casino.
C, Nelson, Barratt, pleasure beach.
D, Whitesands, Wardle, marina.

33 The clerk makes the 18-mile journey (clue 3), so Jason, the storeman, who does not travel 20 miles (clue 1), must live 15 miles from work, and, by elimination, the man who travels 20 miles must be the accountant. This is not Tony (clue 4), so it must be Dennis, who travels by bus (clue 2). Now, by elimination, the clerk must be Tony. From clue 1, Jason does not come by train, so he must use his car, leaving Tony as the traveler by train.

Thus:

Dennis, accountant, 20 miles, bus.
Jason, storeman, 15 miles, car.
Tony, clerk, 18 miles, train.

34

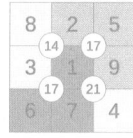

35 Felicity's playing a vampire when she falls from the bridge (clue 2) and the bride falls into a river (clue 4), so the character who falls from the pier into the sea, who isn't a nurse (clue 5), must be a police-woman. The helicopter isn't what the bride falls from into the river (clue 4), so she must go off a balcony, and the helicopter must be what the nurse falls from in *Walkover* (clue 5). The movie in which Felicity falls from the balcony as a bride isn't *Get Lucky* (clue 3), so must be *Outsiders*. Policewoman Felicity's fall from a pier into the sea can't be in *Blue Skies*, in which she falls into a canal (clue 1), so must be in *Get Lucky*, and *Blue Skies* must feature the fall from a bridge, for which Felicity plays a vampire (clue 2). By elimination, when Felicity appears in *Walkover* as a nurse falling from a helicopter she must fall into a lake.

Thus:

> *Blue Skies*, vampire, bridge, canal.
> *Get Lucky*, policewoman, pier, sea.
> *Outsiders*, bride, balcony, river.
> *Walkover*, nurse, helicopter, lake.

36 Aileen provided cookies (clue 3). May did not offer fruit cake (clue 2), so she must have served cupcakes and must therefore have apartment 15 (clue 1). So it must be Gertrude, who played hostess on the 9th (clue 4), who made the fruit çake. The occupant of apartment 24 cannot have done the entertaining on the 23rd (clue 2), nor did the woman from apartment 7 (clue 4), so it must have been May from apartment 15 who was the hostess then, with the woman from apartment 24 officiating on the 16th (clue 2) and the one from apartment 7 on the 9th, which was Gertrude's date (clue 4). By elimination, Aileen must have apartment 24.

Thus:

> Aileen, 16th, cookies, No. 24.
> Gertrude, 9th, fruit cake, No. 7.
> May, 23rd, cupcakes, No. 15.

37 Graphaelo is not the photographer (clue 1). Michelcarlo is the sculptor (clue 3), so Graphaelo must be the painter and Davido the photographer. Graphaelo used flowers as his subject (clue 1), whereas Michelcarlo's artwork did not involve ice cream (clue 3), so it must have been fashion and he is from Milan (clue 2). Leaving ice cream as the subject of Davido's work, so he must be from Naples (clue 3) and Graphaelo is from Rome.

Thus:

Davido, photographer, ice cream, Naples.

Graphaelo, painter, flowers, Rome.

Michelcarlo, sculptor, fashion, Milan.

38 The English teacher loves classical music (clue 3), so Cassandra, the Spanish teacher, who does not like jazz (clue1), must be Jones, who is the pop music fan (clue 4). So, by elimination, the math teacher must love jazz. This teacher's surname is not Douglas (clue 2), so it must be Parnell, leaving the English teacher as Douglas. Parnell is not Daniel (clue 5), so she must be Linda, leaving Daniel's surname as Douglas.

Thus:

Cassandra Jones, Spanish, pop.

Daniel Douglas, English, classical.

Linda Parnell, math, jazz.

39 Bernard's from Australia (clue 1), so the teacher, who is the same gender as the New Zealander (clue 3), can't be Alastair, and isn't Cherry (clue 3). Diana's the doctor (clue 1), so the head teacher must be Bernard from Australia, and the New Zealander is therefore Alastair, whose surname is Houghton (clue 4). From clue 2, Alastair can't be the priest, who must therefore be Cherry, and Alastair must be the clerk. Diana isn't from Canada (clue 2), so she must be from England, and Cherry must be from Canada. Her surname isn't Scott (clue 3), and neither is Diana's, which is one letter longer than Bernard's (clue 1); we know Alastair is Houghton, so Bernard must be Scott, Diana must be Newton (clue 1), and, by elimination, Cherry must be Dugdale.

Thus:

Alastair Houghton, New Zealand, clerk.

Bernard Scott, Australia, teacher.

Cherry Dugdale, Canada, priest.

Diana Newton, England, doctor.

40

	B	D		A	C
D			A	C	B
	C	A	D	B	
A		B	C		D
C	D		B		A
B	A	C		D	

41 Short is wearing the red scarf (clue 2). Bernice High, whose scarf is not yellow (clue 1), cannot be skater 1, whose scarf is blue (clues 1 and 4), so her scarf must be green. We know she is not skater 1, and, since the latter's scarf is blue, clue 1 also rules her out as skater 2, while, from clue 3, she cannot be skater 4, so she must be skater 3. Therefore, from clue 1, skater 2 must have the yellow scarf, and, from clue 3, Louise must be skater 4, who, by elimination, must be wearing the red scarf, so she must be Short. Jackie is not skater 2 (clue 5), so she must be skater 1, and skater 2 must be Charlotte. Jackie is not Long (clue 5), so she must be Little, leaving Long as Charlotte's surname.

Thus:

1, Jackie Little, blue.
2, Charlotte Long, yellow.
3, Bernice High, green.
4, Louise Short, red.

42 "Ginger" Hood is cutting through the side wall (clue 1) and "Rocky" Sikes's target is in North London (clue 4), so the man who's tunneling into the South London building through the floor and who isn't "Spider" Turpin (clue 2), must be "Ozzy" Peace. "Rocky" Sikes's North London target isn't the bank being entered through the back wall (clue 4), so he must be going in through the roof, and, by elimination, the bank being entered through the back wall must be "Spider" Turpin's target. The bank is not in West London, where the art gallery is located (clue 3), and we know it's not in North or South London, so it must be in East London. By elimination, the art gallery in West London must be "Ginger" Hood's target that he's entering through the side wall. "Ozzy" Peace's South London target isn't the bullion dealers (clue 2), so must be the jewelers and, by elimination, the bullion dealers must be "Rocky" Sikes' North London target.

Thus:

"Ginger" Hood, art gallery, West London, side wall.
"Ozzy" Peace, jewelers, South London, floor.
"Rocky" Sikes, bullion dealers, North London, roof.
"Spider" Turpin, bank, East London, back wall.

43 Patsy Peace is the Wise Man's mom (clue 3) and Sue Sikes's child is playing an animal (clue 5), so the shepherd's mom in charge of refreshments, who isn't Helen Hood, Rebecca's mother (clue 1), must be Tracy Turpin. Rebecca Hood isn't playing an ox (clue 1), so she must be playing the donkey, and Sue Sikes's child must be playing the ox. Matthew's mom is in charge of costumes (clue 4), so she can't be Tracy Turpin, who we know is in charge of refreshments, nor is Tracy's child Clive (clue 2), so she must be Louisa. From clue 2, Helen Hood is not playing the piano so she must be the prompter. Patsy Peace isn't Matthew's mom (clue 4), so she must be Clive's, and he's therefore the Wise Man. By elimination, Patsy herself must be playing the piano, and, also by elimination, Sue Sikes's child playing the ox must be Matthew and she herself is in charge of costumes.

Thus:

> Helen Hood, prompter, Rebecca, donkey.
> Patsy Peace, playing piano, Clive, Wise Man.
> Sue Sikes, costumes, Matthew, ox.
> Tracy Turpin, refreshments, Louisa, shepherd.

44 Eileen, in seat 2, did not land on Boardwalk (clue 2). Alicia landed on the Go to Jail square (clue 1), and the player in seat 3 on the Waterworks (clue 4), so Eileen must have landed on Vermont Avenue. We know Alicia is not in seat 3, so, from clue 1, neither she nor Eileen, in seat 2, threw a total of five. Rachel's total was nine (clue 3), so it must have been Kelly whose two dice added up to five. We know she is not in seat 2, and clue 2 rules out seat 4. She cannot be in seat 1, which is next counterclockwise from Eileen (clue 1), so she must be in seat 3, and therefore landed on the Waterworks. Now, from clue 1, Alicia must be in seat 4, and, by elimination, Rachel must be in seat 1, and her throw of nine must have taken her on to Boardwalk. Finally, from clue 2, Eileen's total must have been eight, leaving Alicia's as three.

Thus:

> 1, Rachel, 9, Boardwalk.
> 2, Eileen, 8, Vermont Avenue.
> 3, Kelly, 5, Waterworks.
> 4, Alicia, 3, Go to Jail.

45 The Thursday problem could not have been the accident (clue 1) or the burst water main (clue 4), so must have been the truck shedding its load. The delay on Tuesday could not have been for two hours (clue 1) or one hour (clue 3), so must have been for three. The 4:00 p.m. incident was not on Tuesday (clue 2), nor was the 11:00 a.m. one on that day (clue 3), so the Tuesday problem must have started at 9:00 a.m. The one-hour hold-up started at 4:00 p.m. (clue 2), so the two-hour one must have begun at 11:00 a.m. This was not caused by the shed load (clue 3) or the accident (clue 1), so must have been the burst water main. We know this did not happen on Tuesday, which must therefore have been the day of the accident, with the burst main happening on Wednesday. By elimination, Thursday's hold-up must have been the result of a shed load.

Thus:

Tuesday, 9:00 a.m., accident, three hours.
Wednesday, 11:00 a.m., burst water main, two hours.
Thursday, 4:00 p.m., shed load, one hour.

46

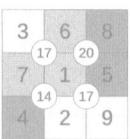

47 Marchant played the doctor (clue 3), and Norbert's surname is Spenlow (clue 2), so Calvin, who played the cab driver (clue1), must be Dreyfus, who starred in the comedy (clue 4). This leaves Norbert Spenlow as the photographer. He was not in the Western (clue 2), so he must have starred in the romance. Now, by elimination, Marchant's first name must be Willard, and the movie he appeared in as a doctor must have been the Western.

Thus:

Calvin Dreyfus, cab driver, comedy.
Norbert Spenlow, photographer, romance.
Willard Marchant, doctor, Western.

48 The channel 8 presenter used to have brown hair (clue 4), so the channel 9 one, who did not have auburn (clue 3), must have had black, and must be Dorka (clue 1). By elimination, the presenter whose natural color was auburn must be on channel 10 and her surname is Voshova (clue 2). Marita's channel cannot therefore be 9 (clue 4) so must be 8. Therefore Dorka's surname must be Rinzova (clue 4). Enya's surname is not Kolorova (clue 3), so must be Voshova and Marita must be Ms. Kolorova.

Thus:

Dorka Rinzova, channel 9, black.
Enya Voshova, channel 10, auburn.
Marita Kolorova, channel 8, brown.

49 Neville is the first name of one of the men pictured in the lower half of the page (clue 2). If Maxwell Bernard (clue 1) also appears in the lower section of the page, then Percy and Gregory would both be at the top of the page, one of those names also being a surname (clue 4). Picture B shows Mr. Lewis (clue 2), so the man in picture A would have to be Mr. Percy, and Mr. Lewis's first name would have to be Gregory. In this case Mr. Percy's first name would have to be either Duncan or Eustace. Clue 3 tells us that this isn't the case, so Maxwell Bernard's picture must be in the top half of the page. Picture B shows Mr. Lewis, so picture A must be the one showing Maxwell Bernard. From clue 4, Percy must be in picture C and Gregory in picture D. One of the men shown in the bottom half of the page must be surnamed Eustace. If this was Gregory, then the other picture would have to show Neville Percy, which it does not (clue 2), so Eustace must be the surname of the man in picture C, whose full name is therefore Percy Eustace, and picture D must show Neville Gregory. By elimination, the forename of Mr. Lewis in picture B must be Duncan.

Thus:

Picture A: Maxwell Bernard.
Picture B: Duncan Lewis.
Picture C: Percy Eustace.
Picture D: Neville Gregory.

50

A			C	B	D
B	D			A	C
	C	A	B	D	
D		B	A		C
C	A	D			B
	B	C	D		A

51 Picture 3 cannot have been taken in Paris (clue 1), Athens (clue 2), or Brussels (clue 4), so it must have been taken in Rome. Therefore it features Anna's cousin (clue 5), and that clue places Judith in picture 2. Now, from clue 1, Anna's sister must be in picture 1, and picture 2 must have been taken in Paris. So Abigail is not in picture 4 (clue 2), and must be in picture 3, taken in Rome. Clue 2 now tells us picture 1 was taken in Athens, leaving picture 4 as the one taken in Brussels. Anna's daughter Lindsay (clue 3) must be the person in this picture, and, by elimination, the name of her sister in picture 1 must be Madeleine, and Judith, in picture 2, must be her aunt.

Thus:

1, sister, Madeleine, Athens.
2, aunt, Judith, Paris.
3, cousin, Abigail, Rome.
4, daughter, Lindsay, Brussels.

52 The gray pony is Bonnie (clue 3), so the brown one owned by Belinda, which is not called Venus (clue 1), must be Pandora. and, by elimination, the black pony must be Venus. Her owner's surname is Hocks (clue 2). We now know that the first name of Pandora's owner is Belinda and the surname of Venus's owner is Hocks, so Felicity Withers (clue 4) must be the owner of the gray, Bonnie. This leaves Camilla as Hocks, and, by elimination, Belinda's surname must be Mayne.

Thus:

Belinda Mayne, Pandora, brown.
Camilla Hocks, Venus, black.
Felicity Withers, Bonnie, gray.

53 Alice Springs is on the May cover (clue 4), so, from clue 3, Pearl Diver and her Hodge can't be on the February or May covers; the same clue tells us that the February pet can't be Cherub, and clue 2 that it can't be Poopsie either, so it must be Nigel. The November pet can't be Poopsie (clue 2) or Cherub (clue 3), so must be Hodge, Pearl Diver's pet, and, from clue 3, the August pet must be Cherub, leaving Poopsie as the May pet belonging to Alice Springs. Since the cat's Nigel, on the February cover (clue 1), from clue 2 his owner must be Rose Busch, and the rabbit must be on the August cover, and so is Cherub. Poopsie, the May pet, isn't a gerbil (clue 4), so must be a parrot, leaving the gerbil as the November

pet, Hodge. By elimination, the August pet, Cherub the rabbit, must belong to Coral Reef.

Thus:

February, Rose Busch, Nigel, cat.
May, Alice Springs, Poopsie, parrot.
August, Coral Reef, Cherub, rabbit.
November, Pearl Diver, Hodge, gerbil.

54

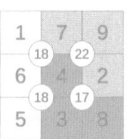

55 Bridget is responsible for the dessert (clue 4). Lottie does not serve the drinks (clue 3), so must serve the main course and Nell, the drinks. So, from clue 2, Lottie must be 56. Nell cannot be 54 (clue 1) so must be 52 and Bridget therefore 54. Lottie has been serving for 18 years (clue 3); Nell's years of experience must be more than 16 (clue 1), so must be 20 and Bridget's, 16.

Thus:

Bridget, 54, 16, dessert.
Lottie, 56, 18, main course.
Nell, 52, 20, drinks.

56 Daisy is pony 4 (clue 3). Pony 1 cannot be Buttercup (clue 1), or Cowslip (clue 5), so it must be Bluebell, ridden by Jennifer (clue 2). The rider of pony 3 is not Melanie Hoofe (clue 4), and we know she is not Jennifer. Clue 1 rules out Loretta, who is immediately in front of Buttercup, so Alison must be on pony 3. We have named ponies 1 and 4. From clue 1, Buttercup cannot be pony 2, so it must be pony 3, ridden by Alison, leaving pony 2 as Cowslip. So Jennifer's surname must be Withers (clue 5), and, from clue 1, Loretta must be riding Cowslip, which leaves Daisy as Melanie Hoofe's pony. Loretta's surname is not Mayne (clue 1), so it must be Hock, leaving Alison's as Mayne.

Thus:
1, Bluebell, Jennifer Withers.
2, Cowslip, Loretta Hock.
3, Buttercup, Alison Mayne.
4, Daisy, Melanie Hoofe.

57 The find on Friday 6th was Fran Grubb's (clue 1), so, from clue 2, Eric Diggs must have made his on Monday 2nd, and it was therefore Saxon (clue 4). It wasn't the brooch (clue 2), the landmine, which was of World War II origin (clue 3), or the helmet (clue 4), so must have been the coins. Therefore, from clue 3, Ann Burrow's find must have been made on Monday 16th, and, by elimination, the Friday 20th find was made by Cary Delve. From clue 3, this must have been the World War II landmine. So, from clue 2, the brooch must have been found on Monday 16th, and, by elimination, the helmet on Friday 6th. The helmet wasn't Roman (clue 1), so must have been Viking, and the Roman item must have been the brooch Ann Burrow found on Monday 16th.

Thus:
Monday 2nd, Eric Diggs, coins, Saxon.
Friday 6th, Fran Grubb, helmet, Viking.
Monday 16th, Ann Burrow, brooch, Roman.
Friday 20th, Cary Delve, landmine, World War II.

58 Pearl went to France (clue 1) and the visitor to Austria broke a leg (clue 2), so Sonia, who broke her collarbone (clue 4), must have done so in Switzerland. By elimination, Pearl must have broken her arm and it must be Delia who went to Austria. Mrs. Stubbs is neither Sonia nor Pearl (clue 3), so she must be Delia. Nor is Sonia Mrs. Tripp (clue 4), so she must be Mrs. Fell, leaving Mrs. Tripp as Pearl.

Thus:
Delia Stubbs, Austria, leg.
Pearl Tripp, France, arm.
Sonia Fell, Switzerland, collarbone.

59 The second place went to the man from the May 2014 cover (clue 1). From clue 4, the winner can't have been Marcus Nash the motocross rider. Nor was he Danny Evans (clue 2) or Gary Handy (clue 3), so he must have been Sam Tomkins. The man on the November 2013 cover wasn't Marcus Nash (clue 4), Sam Tomkins, or Danny Evans (clue 2), so must have been Gary Handy. We know he wasn't first or second, nor was he fourth (clue 4), so he must have been third, and so, from clue 3, second place must have gone to the orienteer. We now know the name or the sport for three of the positions, so Marcus Nash the motocross rider must have come fourth, and, by elimination, the orienteer in second place who was

on the May 2014 cover must have been Danny Evans. Now, from clue 2, the archer must have been on the November 2013 cover, so was third-placed Gary Handy. Therefore winner Sam Tomkins must have been on the February 2014 cover. By elimination, Sam Tomkins's sport must be lugeing, and fourth-placed Marcus Nash the motocross man must have been on the August 2014 cover.

Thus:
First, Sam Tomkins, lugeing, February 2014.
Second, Danny Evans, orienteering, May 2014.
Third, Gary Handy, archery, November 2013.
Fourth, Marcus Nash, motocross, August 2014.

60

	A		B	D	C
	D	A		C	B
B		C	A		D
C			D	B	A
D	C	B		A	
A	B	D	C		

61 Martin's a librarian (clue 4), Collier's the real estate agent (clue 5), and the police officer made the parachute jump (clue 1), so Robert, who isn't Collier and who went scuba diving (clue 2), must be the bus driver. From clue 3, Robert's surname isn't Hancock or Walters, which is Heather's, so he must be Scott. Collier, the real estate agent, didn't fly a glider (clue 5), and we know it was the police officer who made a parachute jump, so Collier must have driven a race car. We know that Heather Walters isn't the librarian, the bus driver, or the real estate agent, so she must be the police officer who made the parachute jump. By elimination, Collier's forename must be Amanda, and Martin the librarian must be Hancock and must have flown a glider.

Thus:

Amanda Collier, real estate agent, drove race car.

Heather Walters, police officer, parachute jump.

Martin Hancock, librarian, flew glider.

Robert Scott, bus driver, went scuba diving.

62 From clue 1, Broad cannot be in seat 4, nor can Short, the media personality, or Long (clue 4), so Large must be. So, from clue 4, Long must be the chairman in seat 3. We now know this is neither Clive nor Broad, so, from clue 1, Clive, who is not Broad, cannot be Large or Long either, and must be Short, the media personality. Ryan is the building contractor (clue 2), so Peter, who is not the auto retailer (clue 3), must be the accountant, leaving the auto retailer as Brendan. He cannot be in position 1 or position 4 (clue 4), and clue 3 now rules out position 2, so he must be Long, the chairman, in seat 3. Now, from clue 4, Clive Short must be in seat 2, leaving Broad in seat 1. He is not Ryan, the building contractor (clue 1), so he must be Peter, the accountant, leaving Ryan, the building contractor, as Large.

Thus:

1, Peter Broad, accountant.

2, Clive Short, media personality.

3, Brendan Long, auto retailer.

4, Ryan Large, building contractor.

63 Pearl's teacher is Mrs. Slater (clue 4), and the girl called Maloney is in Miss Greaves's class (clue 3), so Sinita Kochar (clue 1) must be with Miss Hughes. So she did not play the part of an angel (clue 2), and clue 1 tells us she was not a sheep, so she must have played the role of Mary. By elimination, Pearl's surname must be Abbott, and the girl called Maloney must be Helen. She, too, did not play the role of an angel (clue 2), so she must have been the sheep, leaving the angel as Pearl Abbott.

Thus:

Helen Maloney, sheep, Miss Greaves.
Pearl Abbott, angel, Mrs. Slater.
Sinita Kochar, Mary, Miss Hughes.

64

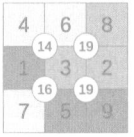

65 Ernie's dog is Tommy (clue 2), and Frank's is the German Shepherd (clue 5), so the owner of Max, the Welsh terrier, who is not Jack (clue 1), must be Dennis. So Max is not at lamppost 4 (clue 3), nor can he be at lamppost 1 (clue 1). Nicko is at lamppost 3 (clue 4), so Max must be at lamppost 2. So, from clue 1, Jack's pet must be at lamppost 1. So his dog is not Nicko, and we know he is not Max or Tommy, so he must be Bruce, leaving Nicko as the German Shepherd at lamppost 3. Now, by elimination, Tommy must be at lamppost 4. He is not the boxer (clue 2), so he must be the Sealyham, leaving the boxer as Bruce.

Thus:

1, Bruce, boxer, Jack.
2, Max, Welsh terrier, Dennis.
3, Nicko, German Shepherd, Frank.
4, Tommy, Sealyham, Ernie.

66 Amanda found a quarter (clue 2), so, from clue 1, Wesley must have found the dime, and the nickle must have been found in the park. By elimination, its finder must have been Joseph. He is not 5 (clue 1), and it was the child aged 6 who made a find on the sidewalk (clue 3), so Joseph must be 7. Amanda did not find her quarter in the parking lot (clue 2), so she must have found it on the sidewalk. Therefore she is 6, which leaves Wesley as 5, and, by elimination, it must have been in the parking lot that he found his dime.

Thus:

Amanda, 6, quarter, sidewalk.
Joseph, 7, nickel, park.
Wesley, 5, dime, parking lot.

67 Andy has enclosure C (clue 2), and the Labrador is in enclosure B (clue 3), so Bugsy, the Airedale (clue 1), must be in either enclosure A or enclosure D. His owners are not in Cyprus (clue 1). The cocker spaniel belongs to the couple in Crete (clue 5), and Bella's owners are in Madeira (clue 4), so, by elimination, Bugsy's owners must have gone to Tenerife. So he is not in enclosure D (clue 2), and must be in enclosure A and, from clue 1, the owners of the Labrador must have gone to Cyprus. We now know Bella, whose owners are in Madeira, is not in any of enclosures A, B, or C, so she must be in enclosure D. Now, by elimination, the Labrador must be Mick, and Andy's owners must be in Crete, so he must be the cocker spaniel, leaving Bella as the Dalmatian.

Thus:

A, Bugsy, Airedale, Tenerife.
B, Mick, Labrador, Cyprus.
C, Andy, Cocker spaniel, Crete.
D, Bella, Dalmatian, Madeira.

68

C	D			B	A
	B	A	C	D	
A		D	B		C
	C	B	A		D
D	A			C	B
B			C	D	A

69 Mrs. Fell's ward is 39 (clue 2). Mrs. Downes is not in ward 53 (clue 3), so must be in ward 47 and Mr. Cropper must therefore be in ward 53. Mrs. Downes had a visit from the Saxenbys (clue 4), so Mr. Cropper's visitors from No. 26 (clue 1), who cannot have been the Dohertys (clue 3), must have been the Ledshams. The Dohertys, whose house number must accordingly be 65 (clue 3), must have paid a visit to Mrs. Fell. By elimination, 81 Cedar Grove must belong to the Saxenbys.

Thus:

Mr. Cropper, ward 53, Ledsham, No. 26.
Mrs. Downes, ward 47, Saxenby, No. 81.
Mrs. Fell, ward 39, Doherty, No. 65.

70 Diana is the teacher (clue 5). Bridget is not the dental receptionist (clue 2), nor can she be the librarian, who leads the file (clues 2 and 4), so she must be Miss Mills, the council clerk (clue 1). The librarian is not Carla (clue 4), and we know she is not Bridget or Diana, so she must be Annette, leaving the dental receptionist as Carla. Now, from clue 3, Miss Sanders must be number 2 in the file. She is not Diana (clue 5), her position rules out Annette, and we know she is not Bridget, so she must be Carla. So, from clue 2, Bridget must be number 3 in the line, leaving Diana as number 4. Her surname is not Langton (clue 5), so it must be Brett, leaving Miss Langton as Annette, the librarian.

Thus:

1, Annette Langton, librarian.
2, Carla Sanders, dental receptionist.
3, Bridget Mills, council clerk.
4, Diana Brett, teacher.

71 June was married at St John's (clue 3), so Diana, who was not married at Holy Trinity (clue 1), must have been married at All Saints. So, by elimination, Megan's wedding must have been at Holy Trinity. Her husband was not Shaun (clue 4), nor was he Rodney (clue 1), so he must have been William, and she was therefore Miss Belfry (clue 2). Diana did not marry Rodney (clue 1), so her husband must have been Shaun, and Rodney must have married June. So Diana was not Miss Hiles (clue 4), and must have been Miss Pugh, leaving the former Miss Hiles as June.

Thus:

Rodney, June Hiles, St John's.
Shaun, Diana Pugh, All Saints.
William, Megan Belfry, Holy Trinity.

72 The Plumbs went to London (clue 2), so the Appletons, who cannot have gone to Paris (clue 1), must have vacationed in Rome. By elimination, the Cranstons must have gone to Paris. They live at No. 13 (clue 4), so the Appletons next door (clue 1) must live at No. 11 and the Plumbs at No. 9. The Plumbs were away for five days (clue 3), so the Appletons must therefore have been away for six days and the Cranstons for four (clue 1).

Thus:

Appletons, No. 11, Rome, six days.
Cranstons, No. 13, Paris, four days.
Plumbs, No. 9, London, five days.

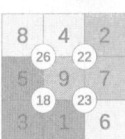

73 Chip Brennan is killed by zombies (clue 3) and the cook by a vampire (clue 1), so Thad Sorino, the guide, who isn't killed by the sasquatch (clue 4), must be the werewolf's victim. Zack Young isn't the cook killed by the vampire (clue 1), so he must be the sasquatch's victim, and, by elimination, the cook must be Jake Keppler. Zack Young is killed on Monday (clue 1), so can't be the sound recordist, who dies on Thursday (clue 2), and must be the cameraman. By elimination, the sound recordist who dies on Thursday must be Chip Brennan. Therefore, from clue 3, Thad Sorino, the werewolf's victim, must die on Wednesday. Finally, by elimination, cook Jake Keppler must die on Tuesday.

Thus:

Chip Brennan, sound recordist, Thursday, zombies.

Jake Keppler, cook, Tuesday, vampire.

Thad Sorino, guide, Wednesday, werewolf.

Zack Young, cameraman, Monday, sasquatch.

75 The first place was achieved in the town sports (clue 4), so trophy B, won at the state meeting for a higher placing than the high jump trophy (clue 3), must have been for second place, and the high jump must be the event for which Karen was awarded third place. The latter isn't trophy A (clue 1), so must be C, and, by elimination, must have been won at the inter-schools sports. If it had been won in May, then, from clue 1, the 1,500 meters trophy would have been won in June, leaving the discus trophy as the one awarded in July. From clue 2, this isn't the case, so the 1,500 meters trophy, which can't have been won in May (clue 1), must have been awarded in July, and third place in the high jump must have been achieved in June (clue 1). From clue 2, the 1,500 meters trophy must be trophy B, leaving A as the one awarded for the discus. By elimination, this must have been awarded in May and must have been for first place at the town sports.

Thus:

A, first place, discus, town, May.

B, second place, 1,500 meters, state, July.

C, third place, high jump, inter-schools, June.

76 Deborah's surname is Vickers (clue 3), so Meg, who is not Mrs. Pearson (clue 4), must be Mrs. Bell, leaving Judy as Mrs. Pearson. Meg Bell has three children (clue 4), so, from clue 1, Bill and his wife must have two. Judy cannot have four children (clue 2), and we know she does not have three, so she must have two, and is therefore Bill's wife, leaving Deborah with four children. Her husband is not Rick (clue 3), so he must be Alan, leaving Rick as Mr. Bell, Meg's husband.

Thus:
Alan and Deborah Vickers, four children.
Bill and Judy Pearson, two children.
Rick and Meg Bell, three children.

77 The Accounts manager wore a dress shirt (clue 2) and one manager wore a T-shirt and shorts (clue 4), so Mr. Cook, who doesn't manage Accounts and wore a kilt but not a sweater (clue 3), must have also worn a beach shirt. The HR manager wore ski pants (clue 1) and Mr. White manages Research (clue 2), so Mr. Cook must manage Sales. The HR manager isn't Ms. Porter (clue 1), so must be Mrs. James and, by elimination, Ms. Porter must be the Accounts manager who wore the dress shirt (clue 2). Mrs. James wore ski pants, so her upper garment can't have been the T-shirt, which went with the shorts (clue 4), so must have been the sweater, and the

T-shirt and shorts must have been worn by Mr. White, the Research manager. By elimination, Ms. Porter must have worn jeans with her dress shirt.

Thus:
Mr. Cook, Sales, beach shirt, kilt.
Mrs. James, HR, sweater, ski pants.
Ms. Porter, Accounts, dress shirt, jeans.
Mr. White, Research, T-shirt, shorts.

78

	A		B	D	C
D	B	C			A
C			A	B	D
	D	B	C	A	
A	C	D			B
B		A	D	C	

79 Passenger 3, who is waiting for a number 18 bus, is not Jack (clue 3). Nor can it be Mark, whose bus has a single-digit number (clue 1), or Harry (clue 2), so it must be Simon Jubb (clue 2), and, from that clue, Harry must be passenger 1. He is not waiting for a number 12 bus (clue 5), nor can Mark be (clue 1), so the number 12's passenger must be Jack. Mark cannot be passenger 4 (clue 1), so he must be passenger 2, leaving Jack as number 4. Now, from clue 1, Harry must be Parkes. Therefore Newell, who will catch the number 7 (clue 4), and who therefore cannot be

Jack, must be Mark. Now, by elimination, Jack must be Archer, and Harry Parkes's bus must be the number 3.

Thus:

1, Harry Parkes, number 3.
2, Mark Newell, number 7.
3, Simon Jubb, number 18.
4, Jack Archer, number 12.

80   The time Alice ordered her cab on Friday was not 2:40 (clue 4) and could not have been 11:15 (clue 1), so must have been 9:20. She visited her chiropractor on Thursday (clue 2) and since she did not go to the hospital on Friday (clue 4), she must have gone there on Tuesday and her Friday journey must have been to the garden center, when her cab was only 5 minutes late (clue 3). The 10 minute wait was not on Thursday (clue 2), so must have been on Tuesday and she must therefore have had to wait 15 minutes on Thursday. She booked her cab for the hospital visit for 2:40 (clue 4), so must have booked it for 11:15 to go to the chiropractor.

Thus:

Tuesday, 2:40, 10 mins, hospital.
Thursday, 11:15, 15 mins, chiropractor.
Friday, 9:20, 5 mins, garden center.

81   Holden A. Gunn is the crime writer and is "seasoned" (clue 1), so this is not his first novel. He did not write *Winter Sun* (clue 1), nor did he write *Diamond in the Rough* as this was a first book, so he must have written *Paradise Green*. Rose Budd is the gardening writer (clue 3), so did not write *Diamond in the Rough* (clue 2). She therefore wrote *Winter Sun*, leaving Fleur Honeysuckle as the author of the romance titled *Diamond in the Rough*, which is her first novel (clue 2). Rose Budd has not had twenty publications (clue 3), so this is her third and the twentieth for Holden A. Gunn.

Thus:

Holden A. Gunn, *Paradise Green*, crime, 20th.
Fleur Honeysuckle, *Diamond in the Rough*, romance, 1st.
Rose Budd, *Winter Sun*, gardening, 3rd.

82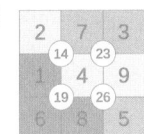

83 Cake 3 was the ginger sponge (clue 4). The chocolate cake cannot have been cake 4 (clue 1), nor, since cake 2 was made by Eileen (clue 3), can it have been cake 1 (clue 1). So it must have been cake 2, made by Eileen. Therefore, from clue 1, the ginger sponge must have been made by Mary, and bought by Thelma. Betty did not make the carrot cake (clue 2), so her cake must have been the lemon sponge, leaving Jean as the woman who made the carrot cake. This was not cake 4 (clue 2), so it must have been cake 1, leaving cake 4 as Betty's lemon sponge. So, from clue 5, Hilary must have bought Eileen's chocolate cake in position 2. Therefore, from clue 2, Linda, who did not buy Jean's carrot cake, must have bought Betty's lemon sponge, leaving Sarah as the woman who bought cake 1.

Thus:

1, carrot, Jean, Sarah.
2, chocolate, Eileen, Hilary.
3, ginger sponge, Mary, Thelma.
4, lemon sponge, Betty, Linda.

84 Penelope did not buy the new dress (clue 2) and she cannot be the woman who treated herself to a new hairdo on Wednesday (clues 2 and 3), so she must be Mrs. Feast, who had the meal in an exclusive restaurant (clue 1). Clue 2 rules out Thursday for Penelope's meal, so she must have treated herself on Friday, and, from clue 2, the new dress must have been bought on Thursday. Ariadne, who is not Mrs. Junkett (clue 4), must be Mrs. Revell, leaving Mrs. Junkett as Daphne. From clue 4, the latter must have treated herself on Wednesday and the former on Thursday.

Thus:

Ariadne Revell, new dress, Thursday.
Daphne Junkett, expensive hairdo, Wednesday.
Penelope Feast, meal out, Friday.

85 David Bell created the picture of Jack Morris (clue 1). Peter Nash's portrait, which will hang in the town clerk's office, isn't the charcoal sketch of Alfred Chinn (clue 3), and clue 4 tells us his subject wasn't Percy Norman, so he must have painted William Moody. Now, from clue 5, the oil painting for the council chamber must show a mayor with eleven letters in his name, so he must be Percy Norman, and, from clue 5, the picture for the mayor's office must show Jack Morris. By elimination, the picture for the entrance hall must be the charcoal sketch of Alfred Chinn. This isn't by Beryl Hunt (clue 3), so must be by Susan Webb, leaving Beryl Hunt as the artist who did Percy Norman in oils. Finally, from clue 2, the watercolor portrait doesn't show William Moody, so must be the picture of Jack Morris by David Bell, and Peter Nash's picture of William Moody must be in acrylics.

Thus:

Alfred Chinn, Susan Webb, charcoal sketch, entrance hall.
Jack Morris, David Bell, watercolor painting, mayor's office.
Percy Norman, Beryl Hunt, oil painting, council chamber.
William Moody, Peter Nash, acrylic painting, town clerk's office.

86

	C		A	B	D
	D	C		A	B
C		B	D		A
B	A	D		C	
A	B		C	D	
D		A	B		C

87 Miranda is the senator (clue 4), and the movie star's surname is Winsford (clue 5), so Julius Benson, who is not the media mogul (clue 1), must be the airline owner. Watson, in position 4 (clue 2), cannot be the media mogul (clue 1), so, by elimination, that must be the surname of the senator, Miranda. Therefore Winsford, the movie star, cannot be Max (clue 3), and must be Davina, leaving Max as Levitt. By elimination, he must be the media mogul. Since he is number 2 (clue 4), from clue 1 Julius Benson must be number 3, leaving Davina Winsford as skier number 1.

Thus:

1, Davina Winsford, movie star.
2, Max Levitt, media mogul.
3, Julius Benson, airline owner.
4, Miranda Watson, senator.

88 Compartment 3 was the fourth to be opened (clue 3), so the animal it features cannot be the tiger (clue 1). Nor can it be the elephant, which appears on the lid of compartment 1 (clue 2), or the lion, which was on the second lid opened (clue 4), so it must be the camel and compartment 3 is therefore red (clue 5). The blue button cannot have been pressed first or third (clue 1), and we know it was not pressed fourth, so it must have been pressed second to reveal the lion, and, from clue 1, the tiger must have been the first animal to be revealed, leaving the elephant as the third. The tiger is not on the lid of compartment 4 (clue 3), so it must be on compartment 2, leaving the lion on compartment 4. Finally, from clue 2, compartment 1 is not green, so it must be yellow, leaving compartment 2 as the green one.

Thus:

1, yellow, elephant, third.
2, green, tiger, first.
3, red, camel, fourth.
4, blue, lion, second.

89 Nurse Hodgson called on Thursday (clue 3), so Nurse Williams, who could not have called on Tuesday (clue 1), must have called on Wednesday and Nurse Lowry therefore on Tuesday, at 10:30 (clue 2) and her first name must therefore be Sharon (clue 1). Nurse Hodgson's first name is not Carolyn (clue 3), so must be Jane and Carolyn must be Nurse Williams. Jane's time was not 10:00 (clue 4), so must have been 9:30 and the 10:00 visit must therefore have been made by Carolyn.

Thus:

Carolyn Williams, Wednesday, 10:00.
Jane Hodgson, Thursday, 9:30.
Sharon Lowry, Tuesday, 10:30.

90 Neither the computer operator (clue 1), nor Ms. Buller, the manager's personal assistant (clue 3), has been with the firm 10 months, so the receptionist must have been. Neither Maxine (clue 1) nor Carol (clue 3) has been there 4 months, so Sheila must have. Therefore she is Mrs. Oxley (clue 2). So she is not the manager's PA or the receptionist, and must be the computer operator, and, by elimination, the receptionist's surname must be Coward. Also by elimination, Ms. Buller, the PA, must have been with the firm 7 months. She is not Carol (clue 3), so she must be Maxine, leaving Carol as Mrs. Coward, the receptionist.

Thus:

Carol Coward, receptionist, 10 months.
Maxine Buller, manager's PA, 7 months.
Sheila Oxley, computer operator, 4 months.

91 The appointment of the man who had had the broken ankle was at 2:20 (clue 1) so that of the one who had had his hip replaced, which could not have been at 2:00 (clue 4), must have been at 2:40 and the 2:00 appointment must therefore have been for the man with knee trouble, John (clue 3). Since Robert's time was not 2:40 (clue 2), it must have been 2:20 and the 2:40 appointment must have been for Ben. From clue 4, Mr. Jonson's first name must be Robert. John's surname is not Milton (clue 3) so must be Burns and Ben's must therefore be Milton.

Thus:

Ben Milton, 2:40, hip.
John Burns, 2:00, knee.
Robert Jonson, 2:20, ankle.

92

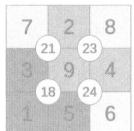

93 Since the head of department is Professor Spriggs (clue 1), from clue 3, Chubb must be the senior lecturer, door D must belong to the lecturer, and the junior lecturer must be Arabella. Darby is male (clue 2), so he cannot be the junior lecturer, Arabella, and, by elimination, must be the lecturer whose study door is D. So, from clue 2, Melissa's door must be C. Also, by elimination, Arabella's surname must be Howlett. We now know her door is not C or D, nor can it be A (clue 4), so it must be door B, and Graham's is therefore door A (clue 4), which leaves Darby, the lecturer, whose door is D, as Jolyon. Finally, from clue 3, Graham is not Chubb, so he must be Professor Spriggs, leaving Chubb, the senior lecturer, as Melissa, whose door is lettered C.

Thus:

A, Graham Spriggs, professor.
B, Arabella Howlett, junior lecturer.
C, Melissa Chubb, senior lecturer.
D, Jolyon Darby, lecturer.

94 The movie is the history (clue 1) and has a female star. Liona Couch is on stage (clue 2), leaving Justin Spotlight in TV. As Justin Spotlight is in comedy (clue 3), Liona Couch must be starring in a tragedy play and Constance Hamm is in the movie. As neither Liona Couch is in London (clue 2) and nor is the movie (clue 1), it must be the TV show starring Justin Spotlight. Constance Hamm is not in New York (clue 4), so must be in Los Angeles, leaving Liona Couch in New York.

Thus:

Constance Hamm, Los Angeles, movie, history.
Justin Spotlight, London, TV, comedy.
Liona Couch, New York, stage, tragedy.

95 O'Sullivan is from Limerick (clue 2) and the man from Galway is a lawyer (clue 4), so Byrne, the journalist, who isn't from Wexford (clue 1), must be from Clare. Therefore he isn't Sean (clue 3). Nor, from clue 1, can he be Barry or Declan, so he must be Pat, and the man from Wexford must be Barry (clue 1). We know that O'Sullivan from Limerick isn't the lawyer or the journalist, nor is he the priest (clue 2), so he must be the neurosurgeon, and, by elimination, Barry from Wexford must be the priest. Barry isn't O'Kelly (clue 3), so, by elimination, he must be MacFeeter, and O'Kelly must be the lawyer from Galway. Finally, from clue 5, O'Sullivan the neurosurgeon isn't Declan, so he must be Sean, and Declan must be O'Kelly from Galway, the lawyer.

Thus:

Barry MacFeeter, Wexford, priest.
Declan O'Kelly, Galway, lawyer.
Pat Byrne, Clare, journalist.
Sean O'Sullivan, Limerick, neurosurgeon.

96

D			A	B	C
B	C	D			A
	B	A		C	D
C	A	B	D		
A			C	D	B
	D	C	B		A

97

Since the goblin was at No. 5 (clue 3), and Delia at No. 17 (clue 5), from clue 1, Pamela, in her witch outfit, and the girl called Cantrip must each have been on the even-numbered side of the street. Since No. 8 was being visited by Miss Fowles (clue 4), this must be Pamela, and Miss Cantrip must have been at No. 22. From clue 2, the latter must have been wearing the snake disguise, and Delia must have been disguised as a dragon. Miss Cantrip is not Caroline (clue 2), so she must be Lesley, leaving Caroline as the goblin. Finally, from clue 5, Delia, who is not Knight, must be Baynes, leaving Caroline's surname as Knight.

Thus:

5, Caroline Knight, goblin.
8, Pamela Fowles, witch.
17, Delia Baynes, dragon.
22, Lesley Cantrip, snake.

98

Newspaper 1 isn't the *Daily Gazette*, the *Daily Journal*, the *Daily Mercury*, or the *Daily Review*, or the *Bulletin* (all clue 2), and from clue 3 it can't be the *Monitor*, so it must be the *Pictorial*. Therefore, from clue 4, newspaper 2 must be the *Daily Mercury* and newspaper 3, the *Daily Review*. Therefore, the *Daily Journal* and the *Monitor* must both be on the front row of the display (clue 3). Since the *Daily Gazette* is next to a newspaper with a one-word name (clue 1), it can't be newspaper 4, which must, by elimination, be the *Bulletin*, and the *Daily Gazette* must be on the front row. From clue 3, it can't be newspaper 6 in the middle of the row, and, if it were newspaper 5, clue 3 would mean that newspaper 6 was the *Daily Journal*, which, from clue 1, it can't be. Therefore the *Daily Journal* must be newspaper 5, newspaper 6 must be the *Monitor*, and newspaper 7 must be the *Daily Gazette*.

Thus:

1, *Pictorial*.
2, *Daily Mercury*.
3, *Daily Review*.
4, *Bulletin*.
5, *Daily Journal*.
6, *Monitor*.
7, *Daily Gazette*.

99 Glyn broke his collarbone (clue 2). Will was not the man who broke his arm in February (clue 3), so Jerry must have been, and Will must have broken his leg. He did not break it in March (clue 4), so he must have done so skiing in January (clue 1), leaving March as the month in which Glyn broke his collarbone. He was not hang gliding at the time (clue 2), so he must have been taking part in motocross, leaving Jerry's broken arm the result of a hang gliding accident in February.

Thus:

Glyn, collarbone, motocross, March.

Jerry, arm, hang gliding, February.

Will, leg, skiing, January.

100 The 10:00 a.m. call was from Vikki (clue 4), and the 12 noon call came from Senegal (clue 2), so Pete's call from Jamaica can't have been at 1:00 p.m. (clue 1) and must have been at 11:00 a.m., and, from clue 1, the doctor must have made the 12 noon call from Senegal. We now know the name or job to go with three of the times, so Mike, the teacher (clue 3), must have phoned at 1:00 p.m. Therefore, by elimination, the doctor in Senegal must be Anna. From clue 5, the call from New Zealand can't have been at 1:00 p.m., and must have been at 10:00 a.m., with the 1:00 p.m. call coming from Kuwait. Finally, from clue 5, the Army officer, who wasn't in New Zealand, must be Pete in Jamaica, and Vikki in New Zealand must be the journalist.

Thus:

10:00 a.m., Vikki, journalist, New Zealand.

11:00 a.m., Pete, Army officer, Jamaica.

12 noon, Anna, doctor, Senegal.

1:00 p.m., Mike, teacher, Kuwait.